withdrawn

THE WHISKY CONNOISSEUR'S COMPANION

Facts, Fables and Folklore
from the World of Whisky

John Lamond

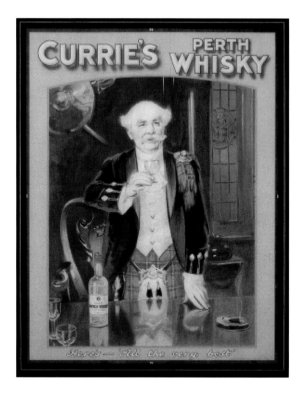

THE WHISKY CONNOISSEUR'S COMPANION

John Lamond

First published in the United Kingdom by The Edinburgh Publishing Company Limited, Admiral House, 30 Maritime Street, Leith, Scotland EH6 6SE

British Library Cataloguing-in-Publication Data.
A catalogue record for this book is available from the British Library.

ISBN 1 872401 11 0

Cover illustration: Courtesy of Perth Museum and Art Gallery

Printed and bound in the United Kingdom by W. & G. Baird

CONTENTS

ACKNOWLEDGEMENTS

A distillate of information, such as this, has an enormous number of sources, many of which have been "tapped" a considerable time, even years, ago. Many of the sources have kindly given permission or help recently, so these are easily remembered. Others, in the mists of memory, are not so readily recalled.

Quotations from the Doncella Book of Pubmanship by kind permission of Imperial Tobacco Limited.

Quotations from *Summer Scotch* by kind permission of The Invergordon Distillers Information Service on Scotch Whisky

Quotations from *The Monarch of the Glen* and *Whisky Galore* by kind permisson of The Society of Authors as the literary representative of the Estate of Sir Compton Mackenzie.

Photographs on pages 6, 8, 9, 16, 20, 22, 28, 36, 38, 40, 42, 50 51, 52, 56, 64, 71, 80, 82, 83, 86, 87, 100, 108, 112 and 115 by kind permission of Moray District Library; and on pages 10, 23 and 129 by kind permission of Perth Museum and Art Gallery

Photograph on page 114 courtesy of The Glenlivet Whisky Co.

Photographs on pages 12, 73, 81, 97 and 104 courtesy of The Glenmorangie Whisky Co., Tain, Ross-shire

Photographs on pages 116 and 130 courtesy of Inver House Distillers, Airdrie

Illustrations by Thomas Rowlandson on pages 7, 25, 43, 65, 89 and 121 by kind permission from *Mr. Rowlandson's England* published by The Antique Collectors' Club.

Photographs on the introduction page and pages 17, 24, 30, 32, 44, 48 and 129 by kind permission of United Distillers.

Picture on page 18 courtesy of Peter Green and Co., Edinburgh.

Picture on page 55 courtesy of Glenturret distillery, Crieff.

Pictures on pages 61 and 106 courtesy of Peter Todd, Todd's Tap, Leith.

Pictures on pages 77, 117 and 126 courtesy of Matthew Gloag, Perth.

Picture on page 94 courtesy of Whyte and Mackay Distillers, Glasgow.

Picture on page 103 courtesy Speyside Cooperage, Craigellachie.

Picture on page 118 courtesy of Messrs. J. and G. Grant, Glenfarclas.

I would like to thank Gordon Brown of *The Guardian*, Ulf Buxrud of The International Wine & Food Society, Malmoe and Kay Botko of The International Wine & Food Society, Minneapolis, Keith Floyd of Floyd's Inn.... Sometimes, Devon, Vince Fusaro of Luvian's Bottle Shop in Cupar, Gill Poulter at Perth Museum and Art Gallery, Alan Robertson of Robertson's in Pitlochry, Joy Thomson of Speyside Cooperage, Graeme Wilson of Moray District Library, Elgin.

...and from the distilling companies: Trevor Cowan of Invergordon, Sheelagh Croskery of Bushmills, Aletta Donaldson and Elaine Bannerman of Matthew Gloag, Ross Gunn of Glenlivet, George Hocknull of Morrison Bowmore, Robin Keillour of Dewar's, Mark Lawson of Chivas Brothers, Des MacFarlane of Guinness Brewing, Carol Anne Night of United Distillers, Jacqui Stacey and Liz Tinlin of Inver House, Kate Stirling of Macdonald & Muir, Jim Turle of Lang Brothers, John Clement Ryan of Irish Distillers Group p.l.c., Richard Paterson of Whyte & Mackay and Peter Fairlie of Glenturret.

For my former colleagues, the staff of Dewar's in Perth who may not be there for much longer.

INTRODUCTION

Five hundred years; five centuries; half of a millenium.

Scotch Whisky has come of age!

It was in 1494 that the Scottish Exchequer Rolls recorded that Friar John Cor was provided with "eight bolls of malt, wherewith to make aquavitae".

What is absolutely certain is that the water of life was produced in Scotland long before this date, but because Gaelic culture and Celtic religion forbade the setting down of knowledge in written form, the oral tradition is virtually the only record of Scottish life and heritage prior to the 15th century.

While the subject is a serious one, your appreciation is very much a subjective and indulgent pleasure. Too many people nowadays are dismissive of comfort and tranquillity. This book should be treated as a bottle of whisky - sup a glass or two in quiet moments. Put your feet up in front of the fire on a long, cold winter's night or relax in the shade during the heat of summer - (if you can find some summer heat in Scotland!)

The tales of Scotch, and Scots, drinking around the world are legion. Many of these stories have passed into folklore, while others fall into the category of fact being stranger than fiction. I have greatly enjoyed my researches into the contemporary records to unearth these gems. I hope that they give you half as much pleasure.

Slainte mhath!

John Lamond

Dewar staff, Calcutta

Leeze me on thee, John Barleycorn,
Thou king o' grain!
                    - Robert Burns.

Cragganmore Distillery, Ballindalloch.

ON THIS DAY IN JANUARY...   *Cragganmore, 1914*

2nd January 1898
- A 9 year old boy dies from severe burns sustained after he falls into a washback at Cragganmore where he is visiting with his uncle.

3rd January 1925
- The Glenlivet distillery celebrates its centenary with a dance which all the staff and neighbouring population attend.

4th January 1655
- Robert Haig is reprimanded by church elders at St. Ninian's Parish Church, Stirling for distilling on the Sabbath.

5th January 1801
- Chivas Brothers Ltd., are founded in Aberdeen.

6th January 1864
- Tommy Dewar (later Lord Forteviot and one of the "Whisky Barons") of John Dewar & Son Ltd., is born.

The man who likes a dram has usually many ways of getting it. An old worthy who was half-seas over had been joining in some national rejoicing when he was met by some friends.

"Well," said one of them, "how are you enjoying yourself, Tam?"

"Man, I'm in an awfu' fix," replied the worthy, "for I started to drink the health o' the Royal Family, an' the funds have collapsed, so I'm stuck at the Duke o' Cambridge."
- William Harvey, *Scottish Life & Character*, 1899.

DRINKING - AFTER ALL WHAT ELSE IS IT FOR?

In days gone by it must have run like water, and it was no uncommon thing for a man to drink a bottle of whisky daily. Lairds and tacksmen had a dram brought to their bedsides before getting up, as their degenerate successors now have a cup of tea - both customs bad, but the former probably the lesser evil of the two. Under the old regime, say forty or fifty years ago, the drinking customs in Skye were notorious. All the tacksmen drank heavily and a whole bottle of whisky only made them mellow
- J.A. Macculloch, *The Misty Isle of Skye*, 1905.

The Hunt Ball

WHISKY IN THE AIR

Alfred Barnard, when visiting Carsebridge Distillery in 1887, recorded that:

"The Distillery was changed into one for raw grain... as though to mark the event, a colony of rooks came and set up an establishment in the big trees which adorn and overhang the Distillery, and there built up a rookery of considerable proportions. At the time of our visit they were very busy, and holding a noisy parliament. The odours of whisky in the air had evidently loosened their tongues, and done them much good.'"

There are three reasons why I drink,
The best; when with good friends, I think;
The second; when I am feeling dry;
Or any other reason why.

-Anon

*The character of Whisky is determined not
by the purity of the spirit manufactured, but
by the impurities left in the spirit.*
                    **- Major Douglas Mackessack of
                           Glen Grant.**

ON THIS DAY IN JANUARY...

Towiemore, 1910

9th January 1840
- Production starts at Glen Albyn distillery.

9th January 1892
- William Robertson, the head maltman at Glen Grant distillery, falls into the grain store at the distillery and suffocates in the moving grain.

10th January 1892
- The roof at Glenspey distillery collapses under the weight of two feet of snow which has fallen over the previous three days.

15th January 1920
- The United States government imposes prohibition on its citizens, a deprivation which is to last almost 14 years.

18th January 1896
- Glenburgie distillery seeks estimates for the erection of the Customs Officer's house at the distillery.

A LOCH LOMOND O' GUID WHISKY

Someone once asked a Highlander what he would wish to have if some kind divinity would give him the three things he liked best. "Weel, for the first," he replied, "I should ask for a Loch Lomond o' guid whisky." "And what for the second?" "A Ben Lomond o' guid sneezin'," replied Donald. "And what for the third?" He hesitated for a long time at this, but at length his face brightened up, and with a pawky look he answered, "Och just anither Loch Lomond o' guid whisky."

- William Harvey, Scottish Life & Character, 1899.

"My father and mother never wanted for company and the house was as full of servants as an Indian or Irish one, strange, ignorant creatures, running in each others way, wondering at the fine English maids who could make so little of them. Amongst the rest was a piper, who, for fear of spoiling the delicacy of the touch of his fingers, declined any work unconnected with whisky, which with plenty of oat-bread and cheese was given to all-comers all day long."

- Memoirs of a Highland Lady.

The old gentleman who used to say that he never drank whisky without water in it was applauded by many for his common sense.
Unfortunately, he usually added that he never drank water without whisky.

A FONDNESS FOR WHISKY

Neil Gow, the famed Scottish fiddler, had a fondness for whisky. After walking home one night to the village of Inver, near Dunkeld, from Perth, where he had been engaged, as usual, to play at some ball, he was asked, next day, how he had got home. It was a long walk of some fourteen miles, and he had been very tipsy. He replied that "he didna mind the length o' the road; it was the breadth o' it that he cast oot wi'!" His recollection was that he had weaved about from side to side. At the end of the 18th century, Gow's fame could be said to rival that of Burns and Neil's strathspeys were on a par in popularity with Robbie's songs.

Banffshire Fiddle Club, visit Glenfiddich, 1897

He who keeps good drink always thrives.
                    - Messrs. J. & J. Grant.

ON THIS DAY IN JANUARY...   *Blair Atholl, 1895*

19th January 1899
- Pattisons Ltd., of Leith goes into liquidation as a result of fraud. This one event is the catalyst which begins almost twenty years of recession in the industry and provides the opportunities for the creation of The Distillers Company Ltd. (D.C.L.).

20th January 1835
- A Royal Warrant is granted to Royal Brackla distillery by King William IV, who "has placed this whisky first on the List of British Spirits."

20th January 1874
- The North of Scotland Malt Distillers' Association, which was to become the Pot Still Malt Distillers' Association in 1925, is established at a meeting held in the Gordon Arms Hotel, Elgin.

24th January 1893
- Mr. P. Mackenzie of Blair Athol distillery feues a site in Dufftown from Provost Symon for the erection of a Dufftown distillery.

"What is it that gives me the necessary sagacity to outwit the Inspector? Whisky. What is it that helps me to know just where to put down the net in Loch Sleeport for Waggett's sea-trout? Whisky. What makes me a good shot at a grouse or a snipe? Whisky. What is it that makes Maclaren such a hell of a good doctor? Whisky. Love makes the world go roun? Not at all. Whisky makes it go roun twice as fast... "

> **- Sir Compton Mackenzie,**
> ***Whisky Galore.***

Scotch Whisky is invaluable in repairing the exhausted forces of nature.

> - William B. Gloag (1826-1896).

THE TRESPASS

An angler fishing a border river had strayed downstream from the beat upon which he had permission to fish. He was challenged by the farmer who owned the beat but engaging the farmer in conversation offered him a dram. "But you don't look as if you were a tee-totaller; will you have a drop of whisky and tell me what you think of it?"

"I dinna care if I do," was the reply: a copious draught was poured out, which quickly disappeared.

"That is good," said the farmer, adding, "it don't burn the throat like some and warms the inside nicely after it's down! Where do you get it?" The angler thus answered the query:

"I get it from Turnbull & Wood of Newcastle; it's called the 'Glen', is patronised by the Prince of Wales and supplied to the House of Lords. It is the best whisky for securing good health and long life ever offered to the public!" The angler then apologised for the trespass stating that he had missed the mark showing the end of the —— Hall water. In apology he offered the farmer some trout which offer was politely declined.

"Then if you won't have some trout, have another drop of whisky," said the angler. As he held the cup in his hand he wished the angler "Good health and good sport," and said, "I am real pleased I have met ye, and will be very glad to see ye come here and fish as often as ye like!"

> - John MacVine, *Sixty-Three Years Angling*, 1891.

Falls on the Bann near Coleraine distillery

*Good Whisky, as a beverage, is the most
wholesome spirit in the world.*
                              - Alfred Barnard.

ON THIS DAY IN JANUARY...   *The men of Tain, 1922*

25th January 1759
- Robert Burns, Scotland's national bard, is born.

26th January 1906
- "What is Whisky?" case.

27th January 1958
- Highland Distillers tell Banffshire Public Health Committee of their intention to open
Glenglassaugh distillery which has not distilled since during World War One. They inform the
council that they will need between 5,000 and 10,000 gallons of water per day.

28th January 1898
- Glendullan distillery receives its first consignment of barley.

30th January 1644
- The Scots Parliament levies the first ever Excise Duty on whisky. This is at the rate of 2s. 8d.
per Scots pint (approximately one third of a modern gallon). The tax was most probably levied
to meet the costs of the Royalist army during the Civil War, 1641 - 1646.

OFF THE DRINK

Some years ago, a butcher and his wife from Scotland's central belt holidayed in the village of Morar on the west coast of Inverness-shire. Being a gregarious couple, they befriended a number of the locals, one of whom was a farmer by the name of Foxy who was fond of the "cratur".

The sassenachs enjoyed, among other drinks, gin and tonic, and introduced Foxy to this cocktail, which he took to readily.

Some months later they returned to the village and walked into the Morar Hotel to be met by a cry from John "the Bar".

"Thank goodness you're back. Foxy has been off the drink since you left."

The couple expressed disbelief at this statement to be informed, "Och yes, he has been drinking your gin and tonic, but he hasn't had a single whisky since you left!"

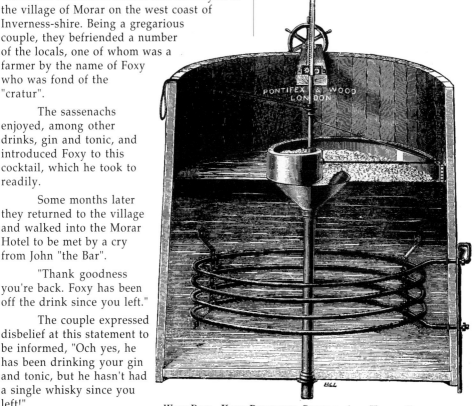

WASH-BACK—YEAST-PARACHUTE, SKIMMER, &c. HASLAM FOUNDRY AND ENGINEERING CO., LTD., DERBY.

There was a large party, chiefly ladies, at dinner. We were very merry during the evening. At last the company retired, and the laird and I were left in confidential talk to enjoy our evening's modicum of whisky toddy.

"Don't take that whisky," said the laird, "try the other."

With this recommendation I complied, remarking that the whisky he had recommended was very mild. "That," he said, "is on account of its age.

- Joseph Mitchell, *Reminiscences of My Life in the Highlands*, 1883.

"I should never have switched from Scotch to Martinis."

- Humphrey Bogart

Oh, Willie brew'd a peck o' maut,
And Rob and Allan cam to pree;
Three blither hearts, that lee-lang night,
Ye wadna find in Christendie.

We are na fou, we're nae that fou,
But just a drappie in our ee;
The cock may craw, the day may daw,
And aye we'll taste the barley bree.

- Robert Burns

KNOCKANDO
PURE SINGLE MALT SCOTCH WHISKY

*K*nockando distillery, situated in the heart of Speyside in the Highlands of Scotland, has been producing fine malt whisky for almost a century.

Built for an independent spirit broker, the first distillation at Knockando took place in 1898. Since then the distillery has only been closed for short periods during the World Wars.

Knockando Single Malt Scotch Whisky is a classic example of the

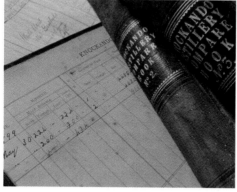

Speyside style of malt whisky: elegant, subtly complex and perfectly balanced. But Knockando is especially delicate and fruity — everything in the production process ensures this.

casks to ensure the naturally delicate flavour of the whisky is not masked. No artificial colouring is ever added. Uniquely, Knockando is not bottled at a predetermined age but rather when the unique profile of the whisky has reached its peak of perfection. The progress of the whisky in cask is followed during the years of maturation, but only Nature knows when the right moment for bottling will be reached. The highest level of craftsmanship is required to recognise this moment.

Each bottle of Knockando records the Season (as a distillation year is known at Knockando) of distillation and the year of bottling. The differ-

Lightly peated barley, the exceptionally pure water of the Cardnach source — only available to Knockando distillery — and yeast are the only ingredients used to make Knockando. Traditional wooden washbacks add their own mysterious contribution. The casks used are of the highest quality; they include only a limited number of sherry

ence between the two dates is the age of the whisky — generally between twelve and fifteen years. Only bottled when at its peak of perfection, Knockando offers the true connoisseur something uniquely special — a single malt possessing the classic elegance and complexity of Speysides with a uniquely delicate and fruity taste.

KNOCKANDO - MAN'S ART, NATURE'S MYSTERY

Morayshire is deluged with excise officials.
                                - Moray Weekly News,
                                        May 10th, 1879.

ON THIS DAY IN JAN/FEB...

*Speyburn distillery
workers, 1935*

30th January 1974
- Production restarts at the rebuilt Caol Ila distillery.

31st January 1898
- Building work is completed at Speyburn distillery by John Hopkins & Co., who later become part of D.C.L. in 1916. Speyburn had the first drum maltings in the pot still industry. The distillery was sold to Inver House Distillers in 1992.

1st February 1896
- Mr. A. Edwards announces his intention to build "a commodious distillery" on the Aultmore property.

1st February 1877
- The first spirit flows from Glenlossie distillery.

3rd February 1900
- Messrs. Alex Fraser & Co. of Glenburgie distillery presents 20 cases of his whisky to Lord Lovat's Scouts who are serving in South Africa during the Boer War. The whisky is especially bottled and a "Tasteful and appropriately designed label" is affixed to the bottles.

CAPTAIN PORTEOUS

On 9th January, 1736 at Pittenweem in Fife, three smugglers robbed an Excise Collector of over £100. All were later arrested, tried and sentenced to death. In these days there was attendance at St. Giles' Church in Edinburgh by such prisoners on the Sunday prior to their execution - this church service was known as "the condemned sermon".

One of the prisoners purposely hit one of the prison warders in church and caused an uproar which was followed by stone-throwing by the mob. A Captain Porteous called out the City Guard after a time and ordered them to fire on the crowd. 16 persons were killed or wounded. Porteous was later lynched and hanged on a dyer's pole. The City Guard was abolished and Porteous' widow was granted £1,500 by the city.

-Perthshire Antiquarian Miscellany

exciseman discovered an open window and poked his head through to see if the distiller was within. Moll grabbed two handfuls of the gauger's beard and held on while her father continued to conceal the casks of uisge beatha. The exciseman roared to be released while the father shouted in English: "Let the gentleman go, Moll" and in the Gaelic: "Keep a grip of him!"

The father alternated between the English and the Gaelic with Moll obeying only the Gaelic instruction until all the evidence was hidden, when their visitor was freed and welcomed at the front door.

NEWLY PLANTED VEGETABLES

The old gentleman who for years managed the boat-house at Perth Harbour bought largely from the shipping smugglers. Having an extensive garden attached to his

Dewar staff, Perth, 1897

The cottage of a smuggling distiller, who worked from home, was "visited" on one occasion by a band of gaugers. The smuggler and his daughter, Moll, struggled to get the evidence hidden away while the excisemen hammered on the door. One prowling

premises, he concealed the ankers (casks) underground and grew vegetables over them. During the smuggling season, the vegetables were often observed to be newly planted.

- Peter Baxter, *Perth, Past & Present*, 1929.

The true smuggler of old exists no longer; he belongs to a bygone age, when what is now considered to be a crime was looked upon as justifiable evasion of undue laws.
                                        - Alfred Barnard

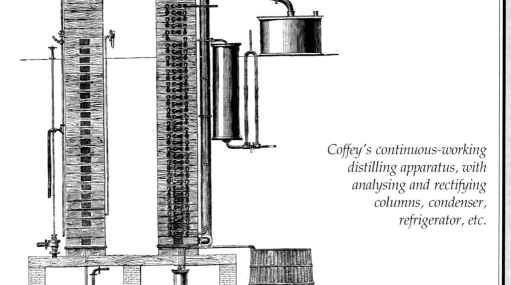

Coffey's continuous-working distilling apparatus, with analysing and rectifying columns, condenser, refrigerator, etc.

ON THIS DAY IN FEBRUARY...

4th February 1897
- The Banffshire Advertiser announces that the West Brewery in Elgin is to be converted into a distillery and to be called Glen Moray.

5th February 1831
- Patent No. 5974 of 1830 - for a continuous still - is granted to Aeneas Coffey of The Dock Distillery, Dublin. Coffey is a former inspector general of Customs and his patent, the "Coffey" or "Patent" still, is the industry standard for grain whisky(ey) production today.

5th February 1901
- Glen Elgin is "exposed for sale at auction", but is withdrawn when it does not reach the upset price of £5,000.

6th February 1605
- Glasgow's Incorporation of Maltmen is sanctioned by Letter of Guildry.

An Abriachan woman was carrying a jar of smuggled whisky into Inverness when she was met near the town by a customs officer who relieved her of her burden.

"Oh, I am nearly fainting," groaned the poor woman. "Give me just one mouthful out of the jar."

The unsuspecting gauger allowed her the desired mouthful which she cleverly squirted into his eyes. She then escaped with the jar before the officer recovered his sight and presence of mind.

- Ian Macdonald,
Smuggling in the Highlands, 1914.

THE BOTHY

An officer came unexpectedly on a bothy and, on entering, the smuggler, who was the sole occupant, calmly asked him, "Did anyone see you comin' in?"

"No," replied the officer innocently. Seizing an axe, the smuggler said, "Ah, then no one will see you goin' out!"

The officer made a hurried exit.

Balfron was a lawless village. It was illicit distillation that demoralised the district. The men of the place resorted to the woods or to the sequestered glens among the Campsie Hills and there distilled whisky, which their wives and daughters took in tin vessels in the form of stays buckled round their waists to sell for a high price at Glasgow.

- The autobiography of Mrs. Eliza
Fletcher (1770-1858).

B. N. J.

BAILIE   NICOL   JARVIE

SCOTCH WHISKY

*Laws against smuggling are generally
disliked.*
               - Osgood Mackenzie.

ON THIS DAY IN FEBRUARY...   *Glenlivet, 1903*

6th February 1975
- The Dark Grains plant opens at The Glenlivet distillery. "Dark Grains" is the term given to the produce of draff, the dried residue from the mash tun, mixed with pot ale, the concentrated residue from the pot still, to give a high protein cattle feed. "Light Grains", being dried draff, is generally sold in pelletised form.

7th February 1901
- Glenburgie distillery is bought at auction by Mr. J.A. Johnston.

8th February 1587
- Mary, Queen of Scots, is beheaded at Fotheringay Castle.

10th February 1905
- Dalwhinnie distillery is sold to Cook & Bernheimer of New York for £1,250.

13th February 1692
- Massacre of Glencoe.

A surviving remnant of the brotherhood, residing near Ballechin, still tells of a halloween night some forty years ago, when the famous Stewart arrived at a place near Perth with a boatload of potheen. He had sent up to the town for assistance to remove the Whisky, when "lo and behold!" instead of his friends, the revenue officers arrived on the scene.

Stewart immediately rowed out midstream, but the officers seeing an idle boat followed him. A chase commenced, and the smuggler, seeing that he was closely pressed and that capture seemed inevitable, proceeded to use strategy that he might escape out of their clutches. Pretending to surrender, he invited the gaugers into his boat to take possession, and seized one of their oars to assist them in stepping aboard.

In a twinkle he had thrown the oar on top of his potheen barrels, and quickly rowed down the stream, leaving the poor discomfited gaugers with but one oar "to paddle their own canoe" as best they could. He was soon lost to sight, and landed his cargo safely in one of his hiding-places on the river side.

- Alfred Barnard, *The Whisky Distilleries of the United Kingdom*, 1887.

NEFARIOUS PRACTICES

In olden days the whole of this district abounded with smugglers' bothies. Our loquacious driver was the grandson of a notorious smuggler, and pointed out to us as we passed, a farm-house perched on the top of a hill, which was the scene of the smuggler's nefarious practices.

On the face of this hill, and just under the farm-house kitchen, was a spacious cave, entered by a small opening made by a dried-up water-course. This they blocked up with stones and pieces of rock, leaving an opening of a few inches wide for the water to trickle through from a spring, which they diverted from the other side of the hill, and brought through the cave. They then burrowed an entrance from a distant thicket, for ingress and egress, and carried a flue from the furnaces some seventy yards underground to the farm-house chimney.

Here for years they made the whisky, whilst their confederate lived in the farmhouse pretending to till the land, but always on guard. In an evil day for them, one of their number, out of revenge, peached to the revenue officers, who made a raid on the place in the middle of the night, broke up the still, tubs, and worm, and took away a few kegs of whisky.

Three only of the smugglers were at work at the time, who were just making up the furnace fire for the night, when a comrade rushed in and informed them that the officers of justice were close upon them. However, as the night was very dark, all four managed to escape, and fled to America.

COPPER STILL, STEAM-JACKETED, SUITABLE FOR GIN DISTILLATION.　　HASLAM FOUNDRY AND ENGINEERING CO., LTD., DERBY
1—Steam-jacketed still body.　2—Head.　3—Spirit-vapour pipe.　4—Worm.　5—Spirit outlet.　6—Steam valve.
7—Spent-wash discharge.　8—Condensed-water outlet.　9—Condensed-steam trap.　10—Manhole.

Copper still,
steel jacketed

Malt Whisky holds within it the climates and characters of Scotland - each one is a distillation of its locality.
                                    - Trevor Cowan.

ON THIS DAY IN FEBRUARY...

Cragganmore distillery in winter

15th February 1980
- Macallan distillery installs a waste heat recovery system.

16th February 1983
- Scottish Malt Distillers announces the closure of 11 distilleries and 2 Dark Grains Plants.

19th February 1894
- Convalmore distillery begins production.

21st February 1895
- The roof of a duty free warehouse at Glen Rothes distillery collapses under "the great weight of snow" lying on it at the time.

WHAT MAKES A SCOTCHMAN HAPPY?

We got at night to Inveraray, where we found an excellent inn. Even here, Dr. Johnson would not change his wet clothes. The prospect of good accommodation cheered us much. We supped well; and after supper, Dr. Johnson, whom I had not seen taste any fermented liquor during all our travels, called for a gill of whisky.

"Come (said he) let me know what it is that makes a Scotchman happy!"

He drank it all but a drop, which I begged him leave to pour into my glass that I might say we had drunk whisky together.

- James Boswell, *The Journal of a Tour to the Hebrides.*

REST AND RESUSCITATION

Wild Highland cattle debate the road with the pilgrim; shaggy collie dogs rush out with wild barks and are recalled by wilder Gaelic curses; men, women, and children gaze cautiously from cottage doors at the hardy stranger who has disturbed their solitudes; it is only five miles to the towers of Armadale, yet you feel yourself in a remote and unknown country. As the inn of Ord is reached, rest and resuscitation in the form of a glass of whisky are most welcome.

- J.A. MacCulloch, *The Misty Isle of Skye*, 1905.

The two Misses ____ kept a carriage, of which they kindly allowed friends to have the use. Charges had lately been carried to the mistresses militating against the sobriety of their old servant, and it was especially insinuated that one public house he never passed without a glass, all of which he specially denied. The Misses ____ had sent the carriage to fetch some friends who, in coming to the house, had to pass the public house in question. Unfortunately, instead of driving straight past, the horses quietly, and in spite of Donald's remonstrances, drew up to the door as if too well accustomed to the process. Donald urged them on the way with whip and voice, bitterly accusing the poor animals of betraying him, "Get on, ye leein' beasts!"

- Dean Ramsay, *Reminiscences of Scottish Life and Character*, 1924.

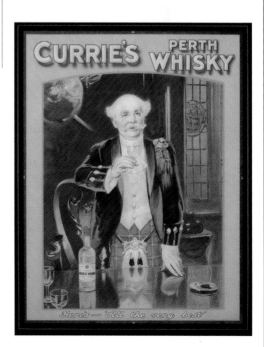

From Greenwich Village to Left Bank cafes;
from sushi bars in Downtown Tokyo to
golfing hotels in the Scottish Highlands, it
(Scotch Whisky) is at home.
                - The Scotch Whisky Association

Benromach, 1962

ON THIS DAY IN FEB/MAR...

25th February 1965
- Moffat distillery produces its first spirit. The malt distillery Glenflagler also sees spirit begin to flow within the same premises. The pot stills have since been removed and Inver House Distillers now produce only grain spirit in Airdrie.

27th February 1919
- Electric light is installed at Cragganmore distillery.

28th February 1898
- Benromach Distillery Company advertises for contractors to build the distillery.

2nd March 1896
- Glenburgie distillery is reprimanded by Elgin County Council for pollution of the Burgie & Kinloss Burns. The disposal of effluent is a great problem for distillers around the end of the 19th century.

Don't Drink and Drive, the sensible advertising slogan used by police forces throughout the world recalls bygone days of slower means of transport when Perthshire farmers met in Perth on Market Day. Many drams were consumed in the course of the day: renewing old acquaintances; sealing contracts; slaking a thirst; celebrating a sale - or a purchase. Fortunately it was the carriage drivers and not the horses which had been drinking as the farmers often fell asleep on their traps or carts and the horses always saw them safely home with no accidents!

John ——, an old carter of the village of Culross, was driving coals one very cold morning to an old lady. When he had delivered the coals, the lady gave him a glass of whisky. After he had finished his glass, John exclaimed, "Aweel my lady, there was never sic a thing in my young days." "What," said the lady in astonishment, "you had no whisky?" "Plenty whisky but never sic a wee gless," replied John.

HYDROPHOBIA

As an instance of acute hydrophobia, it is difficult to surpass the story of the boatman who, while crossing a loch, was asked if the would take some water with his whisky, and replied, "Na, there was a horse drooned at the heid o' the loch twa years ago."

The head of the loch was twenty-four miles distant.

- William Harvey,
Scottish Life & Character, 1899.

A coachman who had driven out the lunch for the beaters on the moor, on being asked if he would like a dram, replied:

"I dinna often tak one; but when I do, it's just aboot this time."

Posting in Scotland

THE SINGLETON OF AUCHROISK
-The Single Malt-

The Singleton is Auchroisk's pride and joy-an unblended single malt whisky of unique character.

The Singleton of Auchroisk is a Speyside malt whisky which is matured for a minimum of ten years. A pure single malt whisky, with its own unique mellow taste.

THE SINGLETON - SOURCE
The very essence of The Singleton's character is a ancient Scottish spring, called Dorie's Well. The pure, crystal clear water, characterised by its' remarkable softness creates the exceptionally smooth taste for which The Singleton is renowned. It is this soft water, cleansed and purified by nature that is The Singleton's life blood.

THE SINGLETON - QUALITY
While nature provides the source of The Singleton's character, it is the unique craft and skill of our distiller that creates the unrivalled quality of flavour and character. The Singleton is distilled in hand-beaten copper stills and matured in specially imported Spanish oak sherry casks for a minimum of ten years. This adds a smoothness to the malt, enhances its rich, deep colour and provides the whisky with its distinctive flavour.

THE SINGLETON - SMOOTHNESS
Oz Clarke - Sunday Express: "There was this one overwhelming sensation- *smoothness* - I'm willing to bet there won't be a gentler whisky on the market."

The underlying taste is pure and very mellow, reflecting the quality and clarity of the water from Dorie's Well. The Singleton has a velvety, nutty character and a fullness and smoothness that comes from ageing in oak. The delicate taste and aroma, without a trace of the harshness of traditional malt whiskies, makes The Singleton a unique and elegant choice.

Oz Clarke - Sunday Express: "Our taste trail finally took us to the Highlands and we singled out The Singleton of Auchroisk as Britain's best single malt whisky. The choice was easy-we were charmed by the warm, smoky flavour."

THE SINGLETON - STYLE
The Singleton is the definitive single malt whisky, which is a stylish and satisfying choice, appealing to unconventional, yet stylish individuals, who are distinguished by their daring life style and innovative outlook. The uncustomary smooth, rich flavour of The Singleton makes it a supremely accessible and approachable drink, ideal for anyone with a distinctive outlook and singular taste.

THE SINGLETON - SUCCESS
The Singleton is a unique, trailblazing malt whisky. It has achieved ten major awards in 6 years, the most recent being:

1992 "Top Malt" - Malt Whisky Association

1992 "Gold Medal" - Monde Selection

1992 "Gold Medal" - International Wine & Spirit Competition.

This clearly illustrates the degree of acclaim it is now enjoying. Now distributed throughout Europe and Japan, The Singleton has achieved celebrity status amongst some of the foremost authorities on the subject of malt whisky.

*Grain, water and science combine to produce
the purest of spirits.*
                        - Invergordon Distillers Group.

ON THIS DAY IN MARCH...   *Aberlour fire engine, 1950*

3rd March 1989
- United Distillers announces plans to inject £12 million into the industry with around £7 million being spent on a new by-products processing plant in Dufftown.

5th March 1790
- Flora Macdonald, who rescued Bonnie Prince Charlie from the clutches of the redcoats of George II, dies.

6th March 1929
- A fire at Glenlossie distillery halts production for the rest of the season. The season normally runs from 1st October to 30th June.

8th March 1911
- Benromach distillery is sold to Harvey McNair & Co., of London.

13th March 1905
- Benromach distillery is given permission by Forres Town Council to "carry a level crossing over the public road into Benromach distillery".

An Excise Officer, anxious to trap an old woman he suspected of shebeening, walked into her parlour, and seeing a bell on the table, rang it, and asked for a glass of milk which was set down before him. After a little he rang again, and asked the woman if she had any Whisky.

"Ay, sir," said she, "we aye have some in the bottle" and set it down before him. He thanked her, laid down a sovereign, which she took, and walked out. After helping himself, he rang again, and asked for his change.

"Change, sir? There's nae change. We ha'e nae license. Fat we gi'e we gi'e in presents; fat we get we tak' in presents; so good-day, sir."

"...thanks to the tied-house system, I have frequently been unable to buy a glass of self-whisky... In many cases, the hotel-keeper, though living in the same town wherein a pot-still distillery was situate, had no idea that he was selling an imitation whisky - he sold what he was supplied with by his principal."

- J.A. Nettleton, *The Manufacture of Whisky and Plain Spirit*, 1913.

Freemasons! to the Major drink -
We daurna speak, but we can wink,
An' heaven be thankit, we can think,
An' thinkin', feel richt frisky, O!
Lang may they thrive in stock an' store,
Balmenach, Craggan an' Minmore,
An' I'll be up to ha'e a splore
In gran' Glenlivet Whisky, O!

- J. Scott Skinner

DRINKING FOR SAFETY

A country laird sent his gardener to bottle a barrel of whisky, and cautioned him to drink one glass before starting so that the fumes might not go to his head. John was a careful man, and took extra precautions, though these were not attended with satisfactory results, and when the laird entered the cellar he found his trusted retainer staggering about the place.

"Ah, John, John," he exclaimed, "you have not acted on my advice, I fear, and failed to take a dram before starting."

"Dram be hang'd!" blurted out John. "It's no' a bit o' use. I ha'e ta'en nearly a dizzen o' them, an' I'm gettin' aye the launger the waur."

- William Harvey, *Scottish Life & Character*, 1899.

Draught horses delivering casks of whisky

In the finest casks, in untouched cellars, the rich flavour mellows and deepens.
                                                      - Anon.

ON THIS DAY IN MARCH...   *Glenlossie stillhouse, 1979*

16th March 1888
- Speyside Distillery Officials' Ball is held in the Masonic Hall, Rothes with "a very large attendance."

17th March 1876
- The Elgin Courant reports that John Duff, the innkeeper at Lhanbryde has entered into negotiations with Lord Seafield for a lease on "a piece of ground at Foths, Birnie with the intention of erecting a distillery." The ultimate result of his negotiations is Glenlossie distillery.

19th March 1800
- Matthew Gloag & Co. were established at 24 Atholl Street, Perth. When Perth held a banquet for Queen Victoria on her first visit to Scotland in 1842, Matthew Gloag supplied the wines.

22nd March 1946
- Hill, Thomson & Co. Ltd., becomes a public company.

23rd March 1940
- Most distilleries cease production due to the grain shortage caused by the war.

SHARING THE FINES

Whisky making was widespread throughout the islands. Tiree alone exported up to three thousand gallons a year.

Since distillation took nearly a month, co-operative work - largely left to the women - was required among the families of a township. Many widows and spinsters distilled for themselves, or gave this service to men of substance, but co-operation was more convenient, for if one operator was caught by an exciseman all shared the payment of the fine and stills, when confiscated, could promptly be replaced. At this time, around 1800, copper stills of ten gallons' capacity could be bought complete with worm, head and arm for under £5 from Campbeltown.

AN HONOURABLE PROFESSION

In July, 1609, on the island of Iona, all the Hebridean chiefs approved nine statutes which helped improve the quality of life for the populace of the western islands. One of these banned the import of wine, but permitted the continuance of the practice of brewing the islanders' own ales. In support of these statutes, the Scottish Privy Council imposed great penalties on the masters of any vessels carrying wine to the Hebrides. The result was that whisky, which had not previously been drunk in any quantity throughout the islands, was now distilled in every clachan - and smuggling became an honourable profession.

Farewell to Islay, a land where our rooms required no locks, our bus driver greeted each passer-by by name, where winter fuel is free for the cutting, where Donnie MacKinnon, brewer of fine Scotch doesn't drink, where the wine, water and whisky are all the same colour, where a "wee dram is always offered to ward of the chill.."

- Kay Botko, *In Quest Of Malt Whiskies* in the International Wine & Food Society's magazine, April, 1991.

THE OUTER ISLES

The Excisemen had an impossible task in the islands. They were not Gaelic speakers and usually had no local knowledge of sea channels. There were no signposts on the land, where the roads were narrow bridle tracks. They were easily misdirected and confounded; their lives were in danger both in encounters with still operators and in encounters with smugglers.

In Lewis, when an officer was offered a glass, it was customary to ask him if he preferred "Coll" or "Gress". These were the townships where the most celebrated of the island's whiskies were distilled.

*If we cannot afford the best, especially in
the matter of Scotch Whisky, then we should
go without it.*
                    - Peter Mackie of White Horse.

ON THIS DAY IN MARCH...   *Dallas Dhu, barrel rolling*

24th March 1951
- George & J.G. Smith Ltd., is incorporated.

26th March 1936
- Hill, Thomson & Co. is incorporated as a private company.

28th March 1986
- United Distillers donates Dallas Dhu distillery to the state to use as a museum of distilling. Although non-productive, the distillery still has all its equipment in place and now forms a part of "The Distillery Trail".

29th March 1926
- John Bisset & Co. Ltd., is incorporated.

THE INCOMER

Although originally from Edinburgh, The minister had served in the west highland parish for thirty-three years and was still considered an "incomer".

John, the beadle, who had served the minister for those thirty-three years, approached him one Sunday after the morning service. "Meenister," he said, "I hope ye dinna mind me saying this, but ye might hae noted that the congregation has been dwindling of late."

"Yes, John, I have noticed. What do you think the reason is?" queried the minister.

"Weel, meenister, your sermons dinna have the same fire and inspiration that they used tae."

"Oh, John, what do you think we can do about it then?" asked the minister.

"I ken ye've been a teetotaler all your life, but next Sunday, perhaps ye should try a wee dram."

The following Sunday, the minister had his dram, conducted the service, preached the sermon and was back in the vestry when John walked in.

"And how was the sermon this week, John?"

"Aye it was better, but the auld fire is still missing."

"Oh, John, and what do you think we can do now?"

"Weel, meenister, I ken yer feelings on whisky, but maybe ye could have twa drams next Sunday."

Next Sunday arrived and while John was in the church - opening the doors, setting out the hymnals and such, the minister had his two drams and thought to himself, "My, that was awfully good." He then proceeded to pour himself a third... and a fourth... and a fifth...

After the service, he was waiting with trepidation for John in the vestry when the door opened.

"Hello John, and how was I this week?" asked the minister, hopefully.

John was full of enthusiasm and excitement, "Meenister, that was the best sermon ye've ever preached, all the auld fire is back again. There are chust two things."

"Oh, John and what are they?"

"First of all, I go up the stairs to your pulpit and open the gate for you, you dinna go rinnin' up the stairs and jump ower it!"

"Oh, I'm sorry John, I'll remember that. What is the other thing?"

"Weel, when ye're preaching the sermon about David and Goliath, David slew Goliath, he didnae knock his bluidy head off!"

THE IMPORTANCE OF DISTILLERIES

For all that the church may have ranted from the pulpit against distilling, distilleries have always been important, if not essential, to the well-being of the community. Caol Ila on Islay had its own Mission Hall, where, until the 1930s, church services were conducted by divinity students from either Glasgow or Edinburgh Universities.

Caol Ila distillery

A TEACHERS DRAM

Back in the 1830's William Teacher, the man behind the premium whisky Teacher's Highland Cream, set about expanding his mother in-laws grocery business in what was then the village of Anderston , just west of Glasgow. By this time the whisky trade was fairly settled and legitimised and looked like having a good commercial feature.

William Teacher realised that by blending, a practice little known until his time, it would be possible to produce a distinctive Scotch whisky that would be constant in quality and flavour. This coincided with Aeneas Coffey, a former excise man who was familiar with whisky manufacturing, revolutionising distilling with the invention of his new patent still, which was able to produce 200 gallons of the purest grain spirit in only one hour.

Being the entrepreneur that he was, William decided to move from selling bottles of whisky over the counter, to shops where the customers could enjoy the taste of a Teachers dram on the premises. The new Dram Shops were so successful that he found himself supplying other retailers with bulk whisky.

Soon William's sons, Adam and William joined the business, which during the Victorian age , was flourishing extremely well. Eighteen licences were acquired in twenty five years, even though the Dram Shops were rather bleak by to-days standards. Shops allowed no smoking and no 'standing of rounds', but for the sum of one silver threepenny piece would supply a liquid said to contain all the ingredients necessary to sustain life. The shops were scrupulously clean, and even a hint of over indulgence would bring one of the hand picked Highland barmen to remove the offender from the premises.

Teacher's Dram Shops were sold around 1960 after serving Glasgow's thirst for over 110 years. The Teacher's Dram Shop pictured here can be seen in Glasgow's Transport Museum, where a typical Glasgow street has been re-created. The street is dated as being Friday 4th December 1938 at 4.30 pm.

*The selection of this picturesque site for a
new distillery is a happy idea, and
thoroughly characteristic of Scottish
enterprise.*
    - *The Northern Scot*, 25th July 1891, on the
            opening of Craigellachie distillery.

ON THIS DAY IN MAR/APR...

Craigellachie distillery, 1920

30th March 1795
- Lowland distillers call for the "total annihilation of Distilling in the Highlands".

1st April 1967
- Rebuilding work is completed at Port Ellen distillery.

1st April 1782
- Andrew Usher is born.

2nd April 1894
- Glenlossie distillery is granted permission to build a tramway to connect the distillery with the railway.

3rd March 1797
- William Glen of the Mains distillery, Linlithgow, is fined for fraudulently operating a still. Within the body of the still is a chamber which collects a part of the distillate and the Customs, therefore, see only a portion of the spirit flowing from it.

Mind ye noo! It's fifteen abave proof and reel dangerous in the hills, it's that soft, and mild, and persuasive! And if ye're no' takin' tent, the young gentlemen will be sitting on a stane out-by on younder moors, and the air will be sae keen, they will never guess its strength, and they'll tak a wee drappie, and then they'll tak an' sit, an' drink, an' drink, an' think it's watter.

- Lady Logan's Memoirs

A HARMLESS ACTIVITY

An Argyllshire farmer was reproved by his minister for engaging in illicit distillation. "Ye mauna ask me," said the smuggler, "to gie it up, for it supports the family. My faither an' his faither afore him made a drappie. The drink is guid - far better for a body than the coarse big still whisky. Besides I permit nae swearin' at the still, an' as all is done decently an' in order, I dinna see muckle harm in it."

- William Harvey, *Scottish Life & Character*, 1899.

DISTILLED IN BOTHIES

Previous to the year 1820 the whisky consumed in Scotland was almost entirely made by Highland smugglers, who distilled it in bothies in the glens among the hills. The Upper Dee and Upper Don were noted for the production of illicit whisky. The evasion of the Excise Laws was not generally looked upon as immoral in those days. The popular sympathy with the smuggler in his warfare with the gauger is shown in the ballads and songs of the day, and notably in the poems of Burns, who laments his own degradation in having "turned a gauger". In Aberdeenshire the trade was conducted by the smugglers with great boldness. There was many a battle or running fight between them and the officers, in which the casualties were sometimes serious and occasionally fatal.

- Alfred Barnard, *The Whisky Distilleries of the United Kingdom*, 1887.

Whisky, drink divine,
Why should drivellers bore us
With the praise of wine
Whilst we've thee before us?
Were it not a shame,
Whilst we gaily fling thee
To our lips of flame,
If we could not sing thee?

Steam-jacketed pot -still, with Corty's Head

Glenlivet, it has castles three,
Drumin, Blairfindy and Deskie,
And also one distillery,
More famous than the castles three.
　　　　　　　　　　　　　- Anon.

Glenfiddich staff, 1923

ON THIS DAY IN APRIL...

4th April 1894
- John Haig & Co. Ltd., is founded.

4th April 1901
- Production starts at Glenlochy distillery.

5th April 1892
- Messrs. Grant of Glenfiddich announces their intention to "erect a new distillery at New Castle of Balvenie".

6th April 1320
- The Declaration of Arbroath (the first Scottish declaration of independence) is signed.

7th April 1715
- The Duke of Gordon leases land at Wester Deskie Glenlivet to Thomas Smith, the grandfather of George Smith who ultimately founds The Glenlivet distillery.

It has unhappily taken possession of the minds of many people that all sorts of grain, wheat, oats, barley and pease are there consumed in great quantities, and that even oat-meal and roots, such as potatoes, turnips, and carrots are made to serve the purposes of distillation; and, consequently, that the markets are really affected by this supposed consumption. Now, the genuine truth is, that no other species of grain are made use of at Canonmills but barley, rye and sometimes such parcels of wheat as happen to receive damage, or are in quality unfit for bread; and that not a grain of oats, pease, or a particle of oat-meal, nor any potatoes, carrots, turnips or other roots are used in the distillery in any shape... So far are the proprietors from consuming roots, that even the cattle and hogs in the distillery are not fed by them. The cattle are brought here to consume the grains or draff and by that food alone they are fattened for market... They are greatly concerned for those unhappy people who suffered upon Friday last, but the nature of the attack made upon their property, must justify them in the defence of it... The people, it is hoped, will reflect that the damage... must be repaired by the publick,

and they have no doubt that the publick will take every measure to prevent further mischief.

- John Haig & Son, Canonmills Distillery, Edinburgh, 8th June, 1894 in a statement to starving rioters.

The ringleaders of the riot were dealt with harshly; two of them were ordered to be publicly whipped through the streets of Edinburgh by the public hangman and banished to the colonies for fourteen years.

"The works, which were formerly corn mills, are of ancient date; as we discovered, from a charter in the archives of the city, that David I conferred them on the Canons of Holyrood, but later on, in the seventeenth century, they came into possession of the Edinburgh Bakers' Corporation, an old fashioned Guild enjoying special privileges. In the year 1881 the premises came into the possession of Mr. Johnstone, who converted them into a Distillery. "

- Alfred Barnard, talking of the Dean Distillery, Edinburgh in 1887.

There are those still living who remember as many as fifty illicit stills in operation in the glen.
                              - The Elgin Courant, **12th December, 1884.**

ON THIS DAY IN APRIL...   *Craigellachie workforce, 1926*

9th April 1939
- The stillhouse at Dallas Dhu distillery is completely burnt out by fire. Consequently, the distillery does not re-open until 1947.

10th April 1874
- The Elgin Courant reports that the old buildings of Linkwood distillery are being pulled down and that new, more extensive buildings are being erected.

11th April 1930
- Tommy Dewar of John Dewar & Sons Ltd., dies.

13th April 1904
- A cottage at Benromach distillery is advertised to let. This is the first sign of a reduction in distillery workforces.

15th April 1992
- The Craigellachie Cooperage's visitor centre is opened to the public.

A high civic functionary of Forres had been chaffing the managing director of one of the furthest-up of the Speyside distilleries as to the future of whisky-making in the Spey valley, when the two new distilleries at Dallasmore and Benromach got underway. The next morning he received the following verses which were also published in the *National Guardian* on 3rd June, 1898 and the *Forres Gazette* on 8th June, 1898:

Say you that the Forres trade is dull?
'Tis only just a little lull;
Just wait you till you fill your mull
With Dallasmore Benromach.

What, can't we sell our barley well?
Just wait again and you shall tell
What prices we so soon shall spell
With Dallasmore and Benromach.

The "Guardian" too, says we've no draff,
But here again we well can laugh.
Wait till the spirits pure you quaff
Of Dallasmore Benromach.

The whisky fever's touched us here,
And now we know there's naught to fear.
We'll make the rest look blooming queer
With Dallasmore Benromach.

Then out upon you poor Strathspey,
And all the rest Glenlivet way;
You'll find it mighty hard to pay
With Dallasmore Benromach.

J.McP.G.

Apparatus for testing original gravity

STILL LIFE

The true alchemy of the distilling art lies in the Pot Still House. Here the very apparatus is almost primeval, with the great swelling globular stills, like kettles, patched and rivetted, piping off to a sudden dwindling spout which pierces the wall of the place and vanishes into the open air beyond. These shapes must be the most ancient recognisable to civilised man.

- Alastair M. Dunnett, *Land of Scotch*, 1953.

Whisky, no doubt, is a devil; but why has
this devil so many worshippers?
                              - Lord Cockburn.

ON THIS DAY IN APRIL...   *Glenlivet, 1950*

16th April 1746
- The last pitched battle to be fought on British soil takes place on Culloden moor.

18th April 1986
- Guinness takes control of D.C.L. after a long takeover battle involving the Argyll Group. The Monopolies & Mergers Commission enforce the sale of several brands, including Claymore and Haig to Whyte & Mackay. Following a protracted court case, Guinness's chief executive serves a prison sentence for fraud.

20th April 1608
- Sir Thomas Phillips Kt. is granted a licence to distill at the Old Bushmills distillery in "the County of Colrane and the Rowte, Co. Antrim". The licence is valid for seven years.

21st April 1848
- "Long John Macdonald" of Ben Nevis distillery presents a cask of whisky to Queen Victoria.

23rd April 1877
- The Distillers Company Limited is registered in Edinburgh.

THE KIRK

In Scotland, as in many of the world's nations, the kirk, or church, still has a great influence on daily life. The kirk in Scotland has many faces, Roman Catholic, Church of Scotland (Presbyterian) and two branches of the Church of Scotland which declared themselves "Free" of that denomination. The Free Churches are very strict and spartan in their service. There is a regional divide between the denominations, for example, one island may be Catholic, where the next one will be Free Church of Scotland and the next Church of Scotland.

"Is there anything more to be put ashore, Donald?" queried the captain of a steamer at a pier in the West Highlands. "Aye, sir," answered Donald, "There's the twa-gallon jar o' whisky for the Established meenister." "For the Established minister, Donald?" said the captain, laughing. "Are ye quite sure it's no' for the Free Kirk minister?" "Quite sir," said Donald cannily. "The Free Kirk meenister aye gets his whisky-jar sent in the middle o' a barrel o' flour!"

- William Harvey, *Scottish Life & Character*, 1899.

THE STOOL OF REPENTANCE

When Robert Haig was called before the kirk session on 4th January, 1655, he had to take up a position in the church of some shame and embarrassment - on the stool of repentance. The entry in the session records of St. Ninian's Parish Church record:

"Compeared Robert Haig being summoned for Sabbath Breaking and Wm. Reid, John Groby, William Harley and Christian Eason, Witnesses. Robert Haig denied he knew any such thing as was laid to his chairge. The witnesses deponed unanimously that they saw the caldron on the fyre, and a stand reiking and that they heard the goodwife say "the lasse has put on the caldron and played some afterwort" and she knew not whether her caldron was befor on the fyre on a Sabbath day and had she been at home it should not have been done (for she was byt presentlie cam'd from Alloway Church). So it being only some pynts of small drink played by a servantlass naither maister nor mistresse accessarie to it upon engadgment of Christian carriage for the future, rebuked before the Session."

The parsonage

That whenever they sat at their revels,
And drank from the golden bowl,
They might remember the donor,
And breathe a prayer for his soul.
                          - Longfellow.

ON THIS DAY IN APRIL...   *Glendullan stills*

24th April 1909
- The Glasgow Herald reports the rumour of an amalgamation between John Dewar & Son Ltd., James Buchanan & Co. Ltd. and John Walker & Sons Ltd. The rumour is officially denied, but "as this is always done in the early stages of amalgamation, no great attention is paid to the denials."

25th April 1898
- Distillation begins at Glendullan.

26th April 1963
- Isle of Jura distillery is opened by Lord Polwarth.

27th April 1956
- Imperial distillery is opened by Mrs. Kathleen Grant of Carron House after re-building. It has been closed since May, 1925.

UNQUALIFIED TRUTHFULNESS

A minister of a Highland parish preached one day on the duty of unqualified truthfulness, and was a little surprised to receive soon after a visit from a parishioner, who was well-known to the gaugers as a maker of "sma' still" whisky.

"I have come to thank ye for your sermon yesterday," he said. "I will aye speak the truth after this." "I am glad to hear you say that," said the minister. "Ye see," continued the other, "this mornin' I got a visit frae a gauger." 'Ha'e ye ony Whusky here?' he asked. 'Oh, ay,' says I, 'nae doot I ha'e some Whusky.' 'And whaur is it?' 'Under the bed,' says I."

The old farmer lay dying. The minister frequently visited him and, the farmhouse being a long distance from the manse, it was usual, especially in bad weather, for the minister to get a small refreshment in the shape of whisky and water. On account of his ailment, the farmer was not allowed any spirits and this sorely grieved him.

The minister was telling the farmer about the place for which he should be preparing. Inquisitive, the farmer asked about what would be found there. These questions, the minister answered as best as his knowledge allowed him.

"An' will there be ony whisky there?" asked the old man eagerly. "Oh! no, John, there will be no thought of whisky there. It won't be required. Men there can live without it altogether." "Ay, maybe," stuttered John, "need it or no need it, I would aye just like to see it on the table."

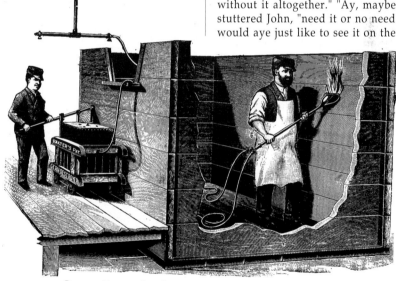

Pneumatic fan-flame germ destroyer

"Weel what dae ye think? I telt naething but the truth, and the cratur never so much as poked his stick under the bed, though he looked through every part o' the hoose. I'm thinkin', sir, ye're quite right; it's aye best tae tell the truth. I maun thank ye for your sermon. It has done me good."

- William Harvey, *Scottish Life and Character*.

Even as late as 1880, the Spirit Act said inter alia: "A distiller must not mash, brew or use a still of any kind between Saturday 11 p.m. and Monday 1 a.m."

BAD WHISKY

It was a characteristically canny remark of a Highlander who, when the minister shook his reverend head towards him, and said,

"Whisky is a bad, bad thing" Donald, replied, "Ay, meenister, especially bad whisky."

- William Harvey, *Scottish Life and Character*.

A FAMILY HISTORY

It has been rightly said that, "it is the whisky they don't use that makes GLENFARCLAS great." Only the finest spirit is selected for maturation

GLENFARCLAS Single Highland Malt Whisky, is known and cherished around the world for it's distinctive flavour.

Born high amongst the snow speckled hills of Speyside in Scotland, the GLENFARCLAS Malt Whisky is the offspring of a miraculous marriage, between location and history. A unique event that has been more than one hundred and fifty years in the making. A dream of liquid gold transformed into the unforgettable taste of GLENFARCLAS Single Highland Malt Whisky.

The Story of GLENFARCLAS is as rich and colourful as the whisky which bears its name. It is a story of one family the Grants, a family united by a single vision-the creation of the perfect malt whisky, the ultimate taste of Scotland; enjoyed everywhere, from the local inns of Speyside to the most exclusive restaurants and hotels in the far flung cities of the world

In 1836 a licence was granted to a small distillery called GLENFARCLAS, at Rechlerich Farm on Ballindalloch Estate, amidst the hill of Moray, but it wasn't until John Grant acquired the tenancy of the farm in 1865 that the distillery began to realise its full potential.

The records and diaries of the family talk of careful men with an eye for the weather and the purse strings. They nurtured the business and were quick to realise that you don't improve on a single malt whisky, you cherish it. A fact of life, appreciated by anyone who has savoured the GLENFARCLAS experience

THE MAGIC OF GLENFARCLAS

Tucked into the gentle meadowland at the foot of the majestic Benrinnes mountain lies GLENFARCLAS-"Glen of the green grassland." This is the home of the GLENFARCLAS Single Highland Malt Whisky, the old great single malt that is the proper pride of Scotland.

High above the distillery a small spring of pure soft, cold, crystal clear water rises from the heart of Benrinnes. This magical well-spring is fed by the slow-melting snow.

The locals will tell you that snow is better than rain. The snow melts gradually, so the water formed seeps unseen through a landscape created by the first glacier movements millions of years ago. This is one of the essential ingredients of GLENFARCLAS Single Highland Malt Whisky.

It is the copper pot still however that makes the whisky great. A good still allows you to tap the lightest and best fractions of the spirit content. GLENFARCLAS is not distilled in a continuous process. It is made with care and meticulous attention in batches. Rigorous controls mean that every batch is as good and as special as the last.

Finally after distillation the whisky is transferred into the finest Spanish sherry casks. Sleeping in the dark cold cellars, the young whisky lies undisturbed for at least 10 years. Only the Angels share the whisky's secret at this stage and only through the natural process of evaporation.

From the oak sherry casks comes the whisky's distinctly rich golden amber colour. When it is eventually poured you will be holding the autumn sun of GLENFARCLAS, transmuted into liquid pleasure, and so it has been for over a century, in fact the only thing about GLENFARCLAS that has been changed in over one hundred and fifty years - is the label.

Considerable investment has ensured that GLENFARCLAS can compete successfully in international markets. A new vatting and bottling complex at Broxburn, near Edinburgh purchased in 1984 meant that for the first time GLENFARCLAS bottling came under the company's own stringent quality control.

THE GLENFARCLAS COLLECTION...
THE PROPER PRIDE OF SCOTLAND

From the cellars of GLENFARCLAS, there comes a superb range or mature single malt whiskies in distinctive packaging reflecting the quality of the product.

Whatever the preference, GLENFARCLAS offers the discerning drinker a unique choice of exceptional quality and smooth distinction.

10 years old...a magnificent Speyside malt whisky, full flavoured, with a slightly dry aroma and a long lingering finish....

12 years old...the popularity of this boldly flavoured malt speaks for itself. It's deep golden - amber colour disguises a slightly mischievous personality. Typically Highland, it has won the praise of connoisseurs across the globe; in particular the Americas have embraced this malt with admiration and awe.

15 years old... "A rich, delicious promise (which is fulfilled)... Full of character and flavour. One of the great Highland Malts." *Wallace Milroy: "Malt Whisky Almanac."*

21 and 25 years old... Distinctively bottled malt whiskies, matured with age for sheer enjoyment...

105... the strongest malt whisky widely available on the market, yet noted for its remarkable smoothness. This is whisky as it was drunk in the 19th Century, straight from the cask.

GLENFARCLAS Single Highland Malt Whisky is not chill filtered - a process which, in the words of John Grant "takes some of the character out of a real malt." Thus GLENFARCLAS is as natural and perfect as the day it leaves its Highland home.

Favoured individuals are allowed to escape entirely.
    - Captain Munro of Teaninich, 30th May, 1823.

Filling casks at Glen Elgin, 1966 - watched by the customs and excise officer

ON THIS DAY IN MAY...

1st May 1707
- Scotland loses its nationhood. The Union of Parliaments takes place and the Scottish Parliament is absorbed into the English Parliament at Westminster.

4th May 1900
- The first spirit flows at Glen Elgin distillery at Longmorn, near Elgin.

7th May 1895
- Messrs. Gordon & Macphail, whisky merchants of Elgin are granted their first retail licence. Gordon & Macphail are one of the small number of independent bottlers who make available to the public whiskies from distilleries whose make is normally used for blending.

8th May 1898
- Lord Kyllachy finds in favour of Glenmoray-Glenlivet Distillery Co. in an action brought by John Milton, a dairyman of Morriston, to prevent the distillery company from diverting the River Lossie in order to use the water for processing purposes.

A REPORT ON SMUGGLING

Landowners had an interest in not carrying the law into effect.

"If a gentleman has an estate in the Highlands worth intrinsically £400 per annum, he may set it to smugglers, if there are mosses on it to supply fire for the purpose of carrying on illicit distillation at five, six, or seven hundred pounds. In like manner the owner of a low country arable farm sells his barley to smugglers at a rate at least one third higher than he should otherwise obtain for it. Even this year barley has fetched from the smugglers in Ross-shire 30s and 32s per boll, while the licensed distillers have bought theirs from Montrose at 18s to 20s."

- Mr. Mackenzie of Ardross in evidence to the Commissioners of a Report on Smuggling, 19th February, 1824.

WHAT A COO!

Some of Sir Wilfrid Lawson's tenants were being entertained one day to dinner. There was plenty of aerated waters and milk for them, but nothing stronger. One of the farmers, who knew by experience what to expect, had provided himself with a flask of whisky, and unknown to a brother farmer poured a generous measure into the glass of milk which his neighbour had elected to drink. In due time the unsuspecting farmer put his glass to his lips, and seemed to enjoy it so that he never stopped till he had finished. Then he turned to his friend and remarked, "Hech! man Thomas, what a coo!

A Highland laird, being unable to maintain a piper permanently, occasionally employed a local musician to play during dinner when he had a party. On one occasion Donald had been overlooked as to his usual dram before commencing to play, and to be revenged played very badly which caused the laird to remonstrate with him and ask the cause.

"It's the bag," explained Donald. "She be very, very hard." "And what will soften it?" demanded his employer. "Och, just whusky," was the reply. The butler, having been sent off for a tumblerful of the specific, Donald quickly drank it off.

"You rascal!" said the laird. "Did you not say it was for the bagpipes?"

"Och, yess, yess," answered the piper," but she will be a very peculiar pipes this. She aye likes the whusky to be blawed in."

- William Harvey, *Scottish Life & Character*, 1899.

Hecking's grains-drying machine

*In this country, scarcely one legal sentence
has been passed for many years!*
**- Sir George Mackenzie of Coul in evidence
to the Commissioners of** *A Report on
Smuggling*, **February 19th, 1824.**

ON THIS DAY IN MAY...   *Mortlach, 1876*

9th May 1877
- A fire "consumed the whole of the premises and distillery proper" at Inverboyndie distillery, Banff. £10,000 of damage is caused, but "the property was only partially insured". It is "afterwards rebuilt on a more modern and commodious plan".

10th May 1719
- Battle of Glenshiel.

12th May 1898
- The Glenlochy-Fort William Distillery Co. Ltd., is established at 51 Church Street, Inverness.

15th May 1922
- Glen Rothes distillery experiences "one of the most disastrous distillery fires in the north of Scotland in recent years" and "a stream of burning whisky" flows out of the affected warehouse.

16th May 1899
- Pollution experiments on distillery waste are carried out in "bacteria beds" at Mortlach distillery.

THE PLEDGE

A Waterford man, who had been drinking too much for his own good was induced to sign the pledge the other day. His wife was delighted. She took the document and said,

"You must let me have it. I will keep it for you." So the paper was confided into her custody. On the next day, the man was drinking as freely as before.

"How is this?" asked a friend. "You signed the pledge yesterday and now you are guzzling whisky again!"

"It's all right," replied the pledge-signer in unsteady tones. "I don't have to keep that pledge. My wife says she'll keep it for me. That's the kind of wife to have. Let's have another drink."

- *Moray & Nairn Express*, 10th April, 1897.

It is a curious fact that the means of producing artificial excitation, or a pleasing flow of animal spirits, is one of the earliest objects of human solitude.

No sooner have herds been domesticated and the land brought into cultivation, than the invention of man discovers the art of preparing an exhilarating beverage.

- Anon 1754.

They were the Golden Folk.
The shining ore
Fashioned their torques and rings and bridle chains,
And brighter than the metal that they wore
Their long braids swung above the chariot reins.
They brimmed their fields with gold, and well they knew
The glint that through the ripened barley runs;
They filled their shells at feasting with the brew
That holds the golden fire of harvest suns.

- The Gaels.

Mortlach staff, 1893

*The lovely little glens with their clear
springs and roaring burns that branch off
from either side of the valley of the Spey, are
one by one being rescued from solitude by
influential companies for the purpose of
whisky distilling, and converted into scenes
of busy industry.*
**- Moray and Nairn Express,
10th April, 1897.**

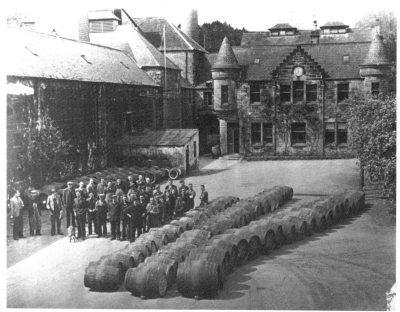

ON THIS DAY IN MAY...   *Glen Grant, May 1953*

17th May 1838
- The purchaser of the Strathisla distillery, having resolved to convert the "Premises into a
Flour Mill" offers the distilling equipment, including the stills and worms, for sale at half
price.

18th May 1897
- The Linkwood-Glenlivet Distillery Co. Ltd., is floated. Distillery buildings, plant and stock
are valued at £42,824 7s. 10d.

19th May 1883
- "The largest still on the premises" of Glen Grant collapses. As a still ages, the thickness of the
copper reduces. The act of distillation, evaporating the liquid, creates a vacuum within it.
When a hole develops in the metal during the distillation process, it implodes, rather than
explodes: the still then collapses.

The whisky was brought down from the mountains, usually during the night, on the pack saddles of ponies or small horses, in single file, to the number of six or a dozen, the halter of the second being tied to the crupper of the first and the third to the second, and so on. The owner usually rode the first horse, and his friends scouted behind and before to give warning of danger from either direction. Sometimes the whisky was captured, and sometimes the smugglers escaped with their booty.

- Alfred Barnard, *The Whisky Distilleries of the United Kingdom*, 1887.

"It is quite a model farmstead, the cowsheds, piggeries, and stables being ranged around a square yard; and we saw upwards of twenty fine head of cattle almost ready for the butcher, and a considerable number of pigs, all fed from the draff or grains from the Distillery."

- Alfred Barnard, describing the farm attached to Annandale Distillery, 1887.

Four be the elements:
Here we assemble 'em
Each of man's world
Or existence an emblem

Press from the lemon
The slow flowing juices -
Bitter is Life
In its lessons and uses!

Bruise the fair sugar lumps -
Nature intended
Her sweet and severe
To be everywhere blended.

Pour the still water -
Unwarning by sound,
Eternity's ocean
Is dark'ning around!

Mingle the Spirit
The life of the bowl -
Man is cold mortar
Unwarmed by a soul.

Drink of the stream
Ere its potency goes -
No bath is refreshing
Except while it glows.

Glendarroch distillery

May the mouse ne'er leave the meal pock wi'
a tear in its e'e
May we never want a freend or a drappie tae
gie him
A willy-waught's a gude night cappy.
                              - Old Scots toasts.

Midleton distillery

ON THIS DAY IN MAY...

21st May 1977
- The Northern Scot reports that the old railway station at Knockando has become the visitor centre at Tamdhu distillery.

23rd May 1872
- James Grant, co-founder of Glen Grant, dies.

24th May 1898
- Forres Town Council grants permission to Benromach distillery to connect with the main sewerage for an annual payment of £8. They are also granted permission to take the water from the Mosset Burn, which is "to be returned unpolluted".

25th May 1963
- The Isle of Jura distillery comes into production after a total refit by Delme Evans.

26th May 1879
- Tallisker (sic) is bought by Roderick Kemp, wine merchant of Elgin, for £1,810 0s. 0d.

THE IMPORTANCE OF CATS

Cats are very important for the health of a working distillery. At any one time, there is a large amount of grain held in store on the premises and this obviously attracts birds and mice - and other scavengers which feast on the grain.

In 1900, for example, Cragganmore distillery on Speyside suffered from "a plague of rats" and Charles Souter, the rat-catcher killed between three and four thousand rats in the September of that year. He had to return in the December to eradicate them completely. The mousers help to dissuade these pests.

TOWSER THE "MOUSER"

On 20th March, 1987, Towser, the "mouser" at Glenturret distillery near Crieff died. Her death created a great deal of media interest, not for the fact that she was only a month short of her 24th birthday - a veritable ripe old age for a feline, but for the fact that she was credited with catching a world record 28,899 mice. Even now, six years after her death, visitors to the distillery ask after Towser.

DIZZY

A young black & white cat from Louisville, Kentucky dozed off among some bourbon barrels which were being prepared for shipment to Chivas Brothers in Keith, Scotland, where they would be used for maturing Scotch Whisky. The cat was unnoticed as the casks were sealed into a 40 foot container for shipment across the Atlantic.

On the container's arrival in Keith on 15th June, 1993, some four weeks later, workers, hearing something moving at the back of the box, immediately abandoned the unloading and shut it up again until the police arrived. The following morning, the cat staggered out of the container, weak through hunger and plastered from the bourbon fumes. He was seized by Grampian police and would normally have been destroyed.

Chivas Brothers offered to pay to have the cat which, for obvious reasons, they called Dizzy, quarantined for six months and, on Dizzy's release from police custody, plan to give him a job as a mouser either at their whisky bond in Keith or at Strathisla distillery.

Towser, World Mousing Champion

A plenteous place is Ireland for hospitable cheer
Where the wholesome fruit is bursting from the yellow barley ear.
                    - Sir Samuel Ferguson.

ON THIS DAY IN MAY/JUN...   *Glentauchers stillhouse*

26th May 1992
- Tomatin distillery opens its £150,000 Distillery Visitor Centre . In the opening ceremony, Scottish Tourist Board chairman, Ian Grant, destroys a limited edition bottle of 25 years old Tomatin with a 22lb. cooper's hammer.

29th May 1897
- The foundation stone is laid at Glentauchers distillery.

29th May 1897
- An action is raised at the court of Session by Mr. Grant of Elchies and Mr. Finlay of Aberlour which estimates that Benrinnes distillery pollutes about 60,000 gallons of the Aberlour Burn every week. The distillers are accused of destroying salmon fishings and spawning beds.

31st May 1991
- Cragganmore donates equipment to be "used in research into the salmon smolt habitat in the upper reaches of the Spey".

1st June 1988
- The Keepers of the Quaich are established. "The Keepers" as they are affectionately known, is an organisation which was formed by several competing distilling companies to promote Scotch Whisky generically. Membership is by invitation only and persons who have made some significant contribution to the promotion of Scotch are invited to become members.

In 1590, it nowhere appears that the Irish then distilled from any description of grain but what had been malted, as the practice of using raw grain is of a much later date. Illicit distillers used only malted grains as from a want of scientific knowledge they conduct their business in a different manner from that pursued by licensed traders.

- Morewood's *History of Inebriating Liquors*, 1838.

SADDLE-SORE

Before the famous coast road was built in the 1830s visitors complained about the ruggedness of the trip. But there was one shining compensation on the journey: the town where tourists made their last stop before the final push to the Causeway was Bushmills. Ever since 1608 saddle-sore travellers have been revived with magnums of the King's whiskey at the world's oldest (legal) distillery which is still in business.

- Northern Ireland Tourist Board.

"As the spirits produced by the Scotch and Irish distillers were of a kind which matured and acquired additional value with age... "

- The Report of the Inland Revenue Commissioners, 1870.

The Spaniard may boast of his shadow,
The Frenchman his sparkling champagne,
But if a man wants to be merry
I'd advise him to try Ould Coleraine.

If you search in the annals of hist'ry
Till the time of the Roman and Dane,
You'll find it was reckon'd a mist'ry
How they made such good stuff in Coleraine.

You've all heard of Barney McCleary,
And the buttermilk waterin' the plain,
And the pitcher, the pride of the dairy
That Kitty got smash'd near Coleraine.

But I'll tell you a saycrit this minit,
I know you won't tell it again
Of milk sorra taste there was in it,
She was smugglin' a drop of Coleraine.

Then hurrah for the trim little boro',
And the Bann as it rushes thro' the plain;
Its waters they banish all sorrow,
When mixed with a drop of Coleraine.

- James Feehan.

Mash house,
Marrowbone Lane
distillery

SPRINGBANK
CAMPBELTOWN
SINGLE MALT SCOTCH WHISKY

The magnificent Springbank, Campbeltown Single Malt Scotch Whisky is unique. Here are just a few of the factors which make it so.

The 'Premier Grand Cru Classé' of Malts
So described by the author of 'Le Livre de l'Amateur du Whisky', a definitive French guide to the great Single Malts, **Springbank** has all the ingredients to justify such a claim: individuality of character, potency of flavour, complexity, and supreme finesse.

Campbeltown
The small burgh of Campbeltown on the Mull of Kintyre was once the 'Whisky capital of Scotland', home to over 20 distilleries; legend has it that the art of whisky distilling was first brought here across the Irish Sea by the monks of the Celtic Church.

Nowadays the number of distilleries has shrunk to two, leaving **Springbank** to share the honour of representing one of the four recognised zones of Scotch Whisky production: the others being Highland (embracing Speyside), Lowland and Islay.

Family Ownership
Founded in 1828, on the site of the previous illicit still of Archibald Mitchell, **Springbank** is the only Scottish distillery of its age which continues in the unbroken ownership of its founder's family.

Proud Independence
Springbank maintains a fierce independence from the many powerful groupings which dominate the Scotch Whisky market. It pursues its own priorities: above all, the making of a highly individual style of Malt Whisky.

Production: An Unbroken Tradition
Every facet of production at **Springbank** remains faithful to its founder's traditions. **Springbank** is made entirely from barley-malt, distilled in pot stills as it was in 1828. The Whisky's colour develops slowly and naturally in oak casks, and is diluted with pure mountain water from the Crosshill Loch.

The Uniqueness of a Single Location
Springbank is the only distillery in Scotland to complete the full production process, from floor malting to bottling, on the single site.

Natural Colour
Springbank is neither 'chill filtered', a process which clarifies whisky at the cost of some loss of flavour, nor is the colour adjusted with caramel: both common practices in the industry. For this reason **Springbank** may vary in colour and turn slightly hazy when cold: better such variances, is the reasoning, than to sacrifice the intrinsic flavour of the product.

A Little Known Secret
A brief study of the map of Scotland will reveal that the road to Campbeltown is a long and winding one. The road to **Springbank** is a similar one, to be travelled by the true connoisseur: but among the mists of the Mull of Kintyre is to be found a rich reward. **Springbank** has received many accolades. Perhaps the most evocative is that from 'Taste Magazine', which describes its "perfect balance and most delicately evocative, though quite substantial, flavour which is at once vivid yet indistinct — like a great Turner seascape".

J & A Mitchell & Co. Ltd., Springbank Distillery, Campbeltown, Argyll, Scotland PA28 6ET
Telephone 0586-552085 or Fax 0586-5523215
SOLE AGENTS FOR ENGLAND AND WALES
Pol Roger Ltd., Lanark House, Ledbury, Herefordshire HR8 2DX.
Telephone 0531-636111 Fax 0351-636146

*There's magic in it. We are working with
nature, with living elements. We are
composers. What could be more satisfying or
creative than that?*
- **Willie MacKay, distiller at Bushmills.**

Still house, John's Lane distillery

ON THIS DAY IN JUNE...

2nd June 1893
- Work starts on the building of Convalmore distillery.

2nd June 1966
- Tamnavulin-Glenlivet distillery produces its first spirit.

3rd June 1899
- The first spirit is run off at Dallas Dhu distillery.

4th June 1784
- Canonmills distillery, Edinburgh is attacked by a starving mob during a famine and is accused of distilling with grain which could be used for bread production.

5th June 1903
- Glen Cawdor distillery is sold to Messrs. Haig & Co. of Markinch for a "purchase price believed to be between £6,000 and £7,000".

HOW "PADDY" GOT ITS NAME

In 1866, Cork Distilleries Company (C.D.C.) was formed by the merger of five old-established distilleries in the Cork area. For years they sold fine whiskeys in cask throughout Munster.

In the 1920s and 30s in rural Ireland, Cork Distilleries' main competitor "Power's Gold Label" began to acquire the reputation of being the best brand of Irish Whiskey. C.D.C. introduced their own distillery-bottled brand which they called "Cork Distilleries Company Old Irish Whiskey".

During the 1920s, C.D.C. had a star salesman in the Munster area whose name was Paddy Flaherty. His arrival into any town on his journey was heralded by a frisson of excitement as he had the reputation of being a generous man, and those who got into the pub first would be included in the round. So well did "Cork Distilleries Company Old Irish Whiskey" sell that publicans often ran low on stock before Paddy came round again on his journey cycle. When they rang the distillery for more stock, they asked for "Paddy Flaherty's whiskey".

The name began to stick. C.D.C.'s directors might have felt upstaged by their employee's success, but were sufficiently commercially-minded gentlemen who recognised a good horse in the paddock when they saw one, and so, one day the name "Paddy Flaherty" appeared at the foot of the label.

A few years passed.

Then the single brand name "Paddy" appeared and thenceforward, although C.D.C. continued to make the whiskey (and to bank the profits) the credit for the brand name has gone to Paddy Flaherty.

"Paddy" is now the number two brand of Irish Whiskey on the Irish market and the leading brand at airport duty-free shops and on board Irish Ferries.

The world's largest Pot Still in the Old Distillery in Midleton, Co. Cork

Air... Water... Earth... Harvest
Transmitted through Copper and Fire and
Wood and Air,
it Becomes the Very Spirit of Place.
                    - Glenlivet advertising, 1992.

ON THIS DAY IN JUNE...

Casks being loaded into Cragganmore's
warehouse for maturation

6th June 1983
- Five men and one woman dressed in costumes of the late 18th century, six highland ponies and twelve casks of whisky, leave Macallan distillery over the old smugglers' route to Perth on a sponsored trek in aid of disabled ex-servicemen.

8th June 1909
- Benromach distillery is advertised for sale by auction "unless previously Sold by Private Bargain". The distillery has known several owners, including National Distillers of America and D.C.L. It was sold in 1992 by United Distillers to Elgin merchants Gordon and Macphail, who intend re-opening and running the distillery.

9th June 1922
- The electric light at Milton (Strathisla) distillery is officially switched on by Miss Mayer of Sunnybrae.

11th May 1896
- George McPherson is fined for operating a "private still".

13th June 1913
- Eight Irish distilleries join forces to form the Distillers Finance Corporation (Limited) with a capitalisation of £1,000,000 with the object of "producing the very best whiskey".

AVAILABLE ON PRESCRIPTION

On 1st March, 1993, the upper house of the U.K. Parliament, the House of Lords, continued a long, and light-hearted (?), fight to have Whisky prescribed as a medicine. To an extent, the fight had been successful in the United States during prohibition, in that some Whiskies, notably those more pungently flavoured ones from the islands, were available on prescription from the doctors. The claim, on this occasion was that, as a medicine, Scotch should not be subject to Value Added Tax.

A schoolmaster who had been appointed to a sparsely populated country district foregathered with a man breaking metal by the road-side, and after interrogating him as to the amenities of the locality in general, proceeded to make inquiries in particular, and asked, "How far is the nearest minister?" "Oh aboot four miles," said the roadman.

"Indeed, and how far are we from a doctor?" "Ten mile and a bittock, e'en as the craw flees," replied the roadman.

"Dear me, that's very awkward. How do you do when anyone turns suddenly ill?" "Och, just gi'e him a gless o' whisky." "But if a glass of whisky has not the desired effect, what then?"

"We just gi'e him anither ane." "But if two will not set him right?" "Weel, just gi'e him three." "But if neither three nor four will cure him?" "Weel then just fill him fu' and put him to his bed." "Yes, but if filling him fu' will not suffice?" "Weel, just let him lie in his bed and drink till he's better."

"Yes, yes my friend, but if whisky administered to him in any quantity will not cure him?" "Och weel the sir," gravely replied the roadman, "if whisky winna cure a man, he's no worth curin', an' may weel be let tae slip."

- William Harvey, *Scottish Life and Character*, 1899.

It helpeth red and duskish eyes. It is good for them that have the falling sickness if they drink it. It cureth the palsy if they be anoynted therewith. It sharpeneth the wit, it restoreth memori. It maketh men merry and preserveth youth. It putteth away francins, ring worms and all spots on the face etc.

It is mervelous profitable for frantic men and such as be meloncoly. It expelleth poison.

The smell thereof burnt, killeth flies and cold creeping beasts. It restoreth wine that is turned or putrified.

It is most wholesome for the stomake, the harte and the liver. It nourisheth blood, it agreeth merveylously and most with men's nature.

It taketh away sadness, pensiveness, it maketh men merri, witti and encreaseth audacitie.

Feeding the kiln

I can drink anything brewed out of barley.
            - Ancient Perth resident, 1929.

W & A GILBEY'S DISTILLERY, STRATHMILL, KEITH, BANFFSHIRE, N.B.

ON THIS DAY IN JUNE...   *Strathmill, 1895*

15th June 1824
- James Stewart takes out the lease on Nethermill farm where he establishes Fettercairn distillery.

16th June 1892
- Glenisla (later called Strathmill) distillery is opened.

16th June 1898
- The first "brew" takes place at Glentauchers distillery.

17th June 1779
- Mr. Justerini advertises that his firm (which later becomes Justerini & Brooks - J & B) has imported some "fine Usquebaugh" into England.

17th June 1989
- Allied Distillers advertise for staff at Glentauchers distillery in order to bring it up to full production.

19th June 1892
- William H. Ross, the architect of The Distillers Company Limited, is born.

EIGHT DRAMS MORE

A farmer was ordered by his doctor to take two fluid ounces of whisky in the course of the day. This seemed precise enough; but unluckily a fluid ounce is equal to eight drams and a dram is one of those ambiguous words of which the English language has a supply. It has two meanings - a "nip" and a few drops. The farmer, not knowing what an ounce was, waited until his son came from school, and, on learning that it contained eight drams, was delighted, and said that the doctor understood his case. He had always had eight drams, but he always wanted eight more.

- William Harvey, *Scottish Life & Character*, 1899.

Willie the barber was suffering from an excess the previous night and, when trimming his hair, he nicked the minister's ear with his scissors. As their eyes met in the barber's mirror, the victim said rebukingly, "It's a great affliction the Whisky, William." "Aye meenister," the barber responded. "It fair mak's the skin awfy tender."

Although among the better classes, dram-drinking in the day-time was reprobated, it was a universal practice to precede the breakfast with a glass of bitters, the bottle being always on the side-board. In the Hebrides the practice is kept up to this day, as an antidote against the moist climate and a stimulant to the appetite, which last was generally unnecessary.

- Joseph Mitchell, *Reminiscences of My Life in the Highlands*, 1883.

Wide was our foresires' lore, but only these,

The Northern Branch, were masters of the old

Dark alchemy that from the barley frees

The last elixir, in whose liquid gold

The essences of shining summers dwell,

The peaty fragrance of the snow-fed burns,

The mystery that none may ever tell,

While still the heather to the hill returns.

- Alastair M. Dunnett, *Land of Scotch*, 1953.

"Whisky is the cure for which there is no disease."

- John Fergus, Deacon Convenor of the Trades House of Glasgow, addressing the Annual Dinner of the Incorporation of Maltmen in Glasgow, 16th November, 1992.

Conversation upon tythes

*E*ach of these two fine malt whiskies has a distinguished pedigree, but each its distinguishing features.

Tobermory, is a traditional island malt with the mellow features of the Hebrides. Deanston is a classic Highland Malt with the resiliant purity of the mountains.

Both have just a hint of sweatness that makes them decidedly pleasant to drink. Both have many admirers in many parts of the world.

Bottled and matured by
Burn Stewart Distillers.
65 Kelburn Street, Glasgow G78 1LD
Telephone 041 880 6155

Sales Office
52 Charles Street, London WIX 8DT
Telephone 071 495 7770

In its own land, whisky is a philosophy, a mystique, an embodiment of primary elements recognisable in the earth and the people.
- **Alastair M. Dunnett,** *Land of Scotch*, **1953.**

ON THIS DAY IN JUN/JUL...

Sikes' hydrometer

23rd June 1725
- The Malt Tax is introduced.

27th June 1990
- Production starts at Kinnvie distillery, Dufftown. This is William Grant & Sons' third distillery in the town which is referred to in the old rhyme, "Rome was built on seven hills, Dufftown was built on seven stills". The seven: Balvenie, Convalmore, Dufftown, Glendullan, Glenfiddich, Mortlach and Pittyvaich are still in production, so therefore there are now eight!

29th June 1798
- The Royal Assent is given to The Scotch Distillery Bill.

30th June 1908
- The Royal Commission on "Whisky and Other Potable Spirits" presents its report to Parliament. The Report is to form the basis of legislation to control whisky production and to define "What is Whisky?".

1st July 1898
- Mashing begins at Imperial distillery.

THE MILK AND THE SPIRIT

A distiller was recently seeking a solution to the problem of bacterial growth on paint in his analytical laboratory. Many samples of paints had been tried over a number of years and the company was on the verge of deciding to tile the room when a paint supplier came up with a new ceramic paint. Robert, the company's painter was instructed to paint an experimental patch on one wall and the results were examined over the following four months.

The paint proved very suitable and the foreman was told by the plant's manager to "have Robbie paint the lab." At which the foreman had to admit to having given Robbie the sack the previous day. The manager was very surprised, as Robbie had always been a very reliable worker and asked why.

He had coated the inside of a milk bottle with the ceramic paint and allowed it to dry. Every day for almost four months, he had left the plant at the end of his shift with a full pint of milk. Finally one of the security guards had asked himself how, if Robbie had come into the plant in the morning and had not left during the day, he had managed to get himself a full pint of milk. Robbie was stopped, the "milk" was examined and found to be neat spirit!

A SHARE OF THE CAKE

Towards the end of the 19th century, the Excise introduced many controls in an endeavour to ensure that they received their "share of the cake". On the subject of the Sikes's Hydrometer which measures the strength of the spirit produced, Nettleton says, in *The Manufacture of Whisky & Plain Spirit*:

"The prominent defects in the instrument have been repeatedly pointed out by writers upon alcoholometry... spirits collected at these high strengths rapidly contract upon cooling, so that when the receivers are emptied and the spirits are run into store vats, and thence into casks (in either of which vessels they may remain, if only for one day, prior to again being gauged), a sensible decrease in bulk is observable with the lowered temperatures, whilst no reciprocal increase in strength is registered by the hydrometer. Similar discrepancies occur with spirits of high strengths sent out warm into a cold warehouse - a constant strength but a diminished bulk."

There is many a reason for drinking

And one has just entered my head;

If a man cannot drink when he's living,

How the hell can he drink when he's dead?

- Anon

DEFINITION

Dr. Wiley, chief of the United States Department of Agriculture in 1907, concluded that the name "Scotch Whisky" should be confined to the product of the pot still.

T A B L E S
TO BE USED
WITH
SIKES'S HYDROMETER.

PART I
FOR ASCERTAINING THE STRENGTH
OF
S P I R I T S
AT TEMPERATURES RANGING FROM
30° TO 100° FAHRENHEIT.

PART II
FOR
DETERMINING THE WEIGHT PER GALLON OF
SPIRITS BY SIKES'S HYDROMETER.

Issued under the authority of the
Commissioners of H.M. Customs and Excise.

STEREOTYPED   EDITION.

LONDON:
PRINTED AND PUBLISHED BY
HIS MAJESTY'S STATIONERY OFFICE.
To be purchased through any Bookseller or directly from
H.M. STATIONERY OFFICE at the following addresses:
IMPERIAL HOUSE, KINGSWAY, LONDON, W.C.2 and
28, ABINGDON STREET, LONDON, S.W.1;
37, PETER STREET, MANCHESTER;
1, ST. ANDREW'S CRESCENT, CARDIFF;
23, FORTH STREET, EDINBURGH;
or from E. PONSONBY, LTD., 116, GRAFTON STREET, DUBLIN.
1920.

Price Four Shillings Net.

Sikes' hydrometer tables

For many years a section of the public, particularly in parts of Scotland and Ireland, has recognised patent-still spirit, without any mixture, under the name of whisky, has purchased it as whisky, no attempt being made by distillers or vendors to conceal the method of distillation.
  - from *The Report of the Royal Commission on Whisky,* **1908.**

The Spirit Safe at Aberlour

ON THIS DAY IN JULY...

5th July 1879
- An explosion at Milton (Strathisla) distillery is caused by a stone coming into contact with the mill during the milling process and igniting the grain.

6th July 1891
- Craigellachie begins production.

8th July 1830
- William Cumming, Grocer of Forres announces that he has just been appointed agent for the Kilnflat distillery. Kilnflat is subsequently renamed Glenburgie-Glenlivet in 1878.

8th July 1895
- George Ballantine & Son receive a Royal Warrant from Queen Victoria as "Purveyors of wine to Her Majesty in Glasgow".

9th July 1898
- Craigellachie stops production "to assist in the diminution of pollution in the season of low water" and "as promised to the proprietors of fishing".

OF WOOD AND STEEL AND SPEAKING TUBES

It is logical to think that, as knowledge expands and materials improve, then production techniques will advance. With an industry as traditional as whisky it seems that a step "forward" is immediately followed by a step "backward"!

The great industrial advances of the late 19th and early 20th century saw distilleries throughout the country move over to stainless steel containers for many processes, as it is more easily cleaned than wood - wood tending to harbour bacteria and therefore being difficult to sterilise. The washback, the vessel in which the fermentation takes place, is a case in point.

Having historically been made of planks of Oregon Pine or Douglas Fir tailored together by coopers, many distillers moved over to steel in the early part of the 20th century. Advanced knowledge brought out the fact that wood is a better insulator and thus gives better heat retention (an important factor in Scotland's inclement climate) than steel and many, if not most distillers, have now gone back to wood. The latest two being Bowmore and Glenrothes. James Lochead, manager of Glenrothes said that stainless steel requires a lot of maintenance, but that the wooden washbacks require "cosseting" to preserve them for up to 30 years.

"We must return, however, to the distillery itself and note one or two of its special features. One of these is that speaking tubes have been introduced, in order to save, as much as possible, waste of time in communication between one part of the works and another. The application of the speaking tubes becomes specially important in one instance, and assume something of the comical. When the mill is bruising the malt, the man in charge of the machine is locked into the apartment in which it is working. This is one of the Excise regulations, the purpose of it being, of course, to prevent him from adding to the malt, or taking away from it. There is a possibility that a man locked into an apartment like this for hours together may become sick - he may let the cylinders squeeze his fingers - anything might befall him, and he might howl till he were black in the face without being able to make himself heard above the noise of the mill. At Linkwood he has a speaking tube into his prison."

- *The Elgin Courant*, 10th April, 1874.

I was not aware that highly rectified spirit was so generally used for whisky. One of the most important features of the examination of these samples is that it affords evidence that an economic process is going on by which patent-still spirit is gradually replacing pot-still spirit.

- James Bell in evidence to the Commission on British and Foreign Spirits, 1889, referring to an occasion when he was called upon to analyse some samples of Whiskies from public houses.

Measuring the gravity of the wash at Linkwood distillery

On no account reduce the barley for whisky.
This takes years to mature and is an
invaluable export and dollar producer.
Having regard to all our other difficulties
about export, it would be most improvident
not to preserve this characteristic
British element of ascendancy.

- Winston Churchill during rationing
after the Second World War.

ON THIS DAY IN JULY...

Canal Wharf, Port Dundas distillery

12th July 1897
- Provost Grant of Elgin performs the ceremony of turning on the first mashing at Tamdhu distillery.

12th July 1922
- Messrs. Alex. Wilson & Co. celebrates the centenary of Inchgower distillery (it was called Tochineal until 1871).

13th July 1898
- The plans for the building of Ben Romach (sic) distillery are passed by the Dean of Guildry Court.

13th July 1898
- Glenkinchie Distillery Co. Ltd., Pencaitland, Clydesdale Distillery Company Ltd., Wishaw, A. & J. Dawson Ltd., of St. Magdalene distillery, Linlithgow, Rosebank Distillery Ltd., and William Young & Company Ltd., of the Grange distillery, Burntisland amalgamate to form a lowland whisky combine (which is to become Scottish Malt Distillers Ltd.) with a capitalisation of £300,000.

THE GRAIN

This is whisky in its purest and most wholesome form. It is distilled in Coffey's still, which is acknowledged to be the most scientific form of still yet invented, and is noted for its freedom from fusel oil. Nothing but the very finest grain and malted barley is employed in its manufacture, and it is the healthiest of all whiskies to drink.

- From the label on a bottle of Cambus Scotch Grain Whisky, 1906.

...for bear and bigg is chiefly raised in the Highlands of Scotland; and, if the growers do not find a market at home, as usual, by distillation, the quality of grain is such, that it will not sell in the southern parts of the kingdom.

- From the minutes of a meeting of the Freeholders, Justices of the Peace and Commissioners of Supply of the County of Cromarty, 6th April, 1808

(Bear and bigg were inferior strains of barley which were suitable for growing in the Scottish climate at that time and traditionally were used for whisky production).

One of these orthodox tenets applied to whisky, and it was invariably accepted, as beyond question, that Highland whisky was made solely from malted barley which had been dried over a peat fire, the barley being home-grown, and that pot-stills, heated by furnaces, were used in the distillation. Lowland whisky, one was instructed, was similarly made, except for the peat on the malt-kiln. Irish whisky was treble-distilled in pot-stills heated by furnaces, and the mashing materials were malted barley, with barley and oats, all grain being home-grown. Such an article as English whisky was undreamt of.

J.A. Nettleton, *The Manufacture of Whisky and Plain Spirit*, 1913.

Each consignment of barley is carefully checked by Glenmorangie distillery manager, Gordon Smart (1921-1970)

English spirits, although made from the finest materials, could not, from the grossness and richness of the wash, be rendered palatable or saleable without undergoing rectification to remove their coarseness and harshness.

- Alfred Barnard

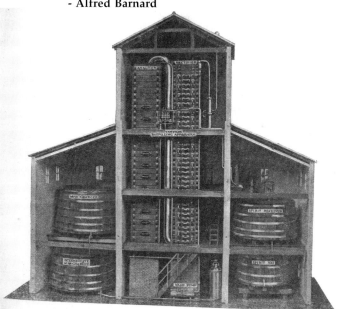

Another illustration of a Coffey Still, with accompanying receiver, etc.

ON THIS DAY IN JULY...

15th July 1864
- William Smith, the distiller at Benrinnes goes into bankruptcy.

15th July 1887
- 25 waggons containing over 16,000 gallons of whisky are despatched via Aberdeen for Dundee.

18th July 1823
- The Excise Act becomes law in the U.K.

19th July 1974
- Auchroisk distillery is officially opened by E.C. commissioner George Thomson.

22nd July 1706
- The Treaty of Union between Scotland and England is signed.

ON OAK CASKS

An oak cask is an essential element in the maturation of Scotch Whisky. It was not always so. Prior to 1908, when it was written into the U.K.'s laws, it was only the wealthy who could afford to age their whiskies. Lloyd George, the prime minister of the time, wished to curtail consumption and saw this as a method of achieving this aim.

At the time, all sherry sold in the U.K. was imported in bulk (in casks). After the sherry had been bottled, the casks were surplus to requirements and the whisky distillers picked them up relatively cheaply.

Likewise, the cooper's union in the U.S.A. was strong when the laws governing Bourbon production were being drawn up and they ensured that the legislation would only allow a Bourbon cask to be used once. Again, once the Bourbon was bottled, the casks were surplus to the American distillers' requirements and the Scotch, and Irish, distillers picked them up cheaply. Since 1983, the Spanish government has legislated that all Sherry must be bottled in Spain. This has greatly increased the distillers' costs.

A cask, being wooden, allows evaporation, or breathing through the pores of the wood. This evaporation, which amounts to 2% per annum, is a necessary part of the development of the spirit's flavour. The cask can have an active working life of 40 years, during which time, the whisky is taking flavour elements from the wood and evaporating through the pores in the oak. It is not unknown for a cask still to be in use after 80 years, but beyond 40 years it is merely an oxidisation vehicle.

At the end of its life, the cask is not wasted - the Scots are a "canny" people. It is reduced to shavings, which are then burnt to flavour Scottish smoked salmon or Arbroath smokies.

The Speyside Cooperage at Craigellachie, in the very heart of Speyside, has been run by three generations of the Taylor family. In 1992 the business moved to new premises on the south side of the village and created an exhibition which they named "Acorn to Cask". This is a modern "living" style of exhibition where the history of the cooper's trade is shown in sound - and smell!

The importance of casks to many industries, other than the Scotch Whisky, (including the world's first submarine, which was built by coopers) is emphasised. There is also a viewing gallery around the working cooperage where they make and repair over 100,000 whisky casks each year. The coopers form a part of the exhibit themselves.

THE DRUNKARD'S CLOAK

In bygone days, someone found guilty of drunkeness at a Burgh court was fitted with and had to wear a cask known as a "drunkard's cloak". A fitting punishment!

Paint used for marking cask end, encrusting the paint pot and its holder

*...in any part of the world where a person
wants to buy the best, the top quality of the
distiller's art, he asks for "Scotch".*
    - Alastair M. Dunnet, *The Land of
                    Scotch,* **1953.**

Inchgower distillery, courtyard

ON THIS DAY IN JULY...

22nd July 1872
- Work is started on the Jones Road Distillery, Dublin. Alfred Barnard describes it as "the most modern of the Distilleries in Dublin" when he visited Ireland in 1887.

23rd July 1965
- The first spirit flows from Tomintoul distillery.

24th July 1891
- Craigellachie distillery "in full operation".

Peat cutting, Orkney

THE PEAT

Having passed acres of peat fields with their ever-present peat-cutting machines and the island's rough-edged, furrowed fields (looking like thousands of moles have been working overtime), the furnaces of Port Ellen reflected the importance of this vast resource. The unique aroma of peat filled the air around the malting facility. The intense heat, long, slow-burning quality and virtual unlimited supply of peat was the strongest impression of this facility.

- Kay Botko, *In Quest Of Malt Whiskies*, in the International Wine & Food Society's magazine, April, 1991.

And drank it round and round,

And still the more and more they drank,

Their joy did more abound.

John Barleycorn was a hero bold,

Of noble enterprise;

For if you do but taste his blood,

'Twill make your courage rise.

'Twill make a man forget his woe;

'Twill heighten all his joy:

'Twill make the widow's heart to sing,

Though the tear were in her eye.

Then let us toast John Barleycorn,

Each man a glass in hand;

And may his great posterity

Ne'er fail in old Scotland!

- Anon

A FERTILE BRAIN

We observed a short time ago a new kind of traffic at our Lossiemouth harbour that encouraged some inquiries concerning it - a ship coming in with a cargo of peats. What could this mean? We have the mosses at Dallas and Kellas beside us, the hill of Auldmore not thirty miles away and the famous Faemusach not at a much greater distance. Peats from any of these almost exhaustless stores of them coming to us either by road or rail would have created no surprise. But peats by sea? The fertile brain of the much-respected distiller at Miltonduff was soon discovered in it. He is the principal partner of Messrs. Stuart & Mackay of Highland Park Distillery in Orkney as well as the distiller at Miltonduff. Encouraged by the success attained at Highland Park in giving the whisky there a creamy thickness, the rich flavour, and fine tone that connoisseurs so much desire in their favourite beverage, Mr. Stuart two years ago resolved to adopt the same style of manufacture at Miltonduff as he and his partner have followed in Orkney.
...procuring the same peats to dry the malt in Moray that do the same duty in Orkney.

- *The Elgin Courant*, 12th December, 1884.

Oh that the peats would cut themselves,

The fish shump on the shore,

And that we all in bed might lie

For aye and evermore, och, och!

- Old Skye verse (from the Gaelic)

HIGHLAND.
An almost feminine charm and character all of its own. Light and aromatic, the Gentle Spirit is rich in body with a soft heather honey finish.

ISLE OF SKYE.
Assertive but not heavy. Fully flavoured with a pungent, peaty ruggedness. It explodes on the palate and lingers on. Well balanced. A sweetish seaweedy aroma.

SPEYSIDE.
Finely balanced with a dry, rather delicate aroma, good firm body and a smoky finish. A pleasantly austere malt of great distinction with a character all its own.

WEST HIGHLAND.
Oban is the West Highland malt. A singular, rich and complex malt with the merest suggestion of peat in the aroma, slightly smoky with a long smooth finish.

ISLE OF ISLAY.
Seaweed, peat, smoke and earth are all elements of the assertive Islay character. Pungent, an intensely dry 16 year old malt with a firm robust body and powerful aroma.

LOWLAND.
Typically soft, restrained and with a touch of sweetness. An exceptionally pale smooth malt which, experts agree, reaches perfection at 10 years maturity.

CLASSIC MALTS
SIX OF SCOTLANDS FINEST MALT WHISKIES

Les grands crus de Scotland.

In the great wine-growing regions, there are certain growths from a single estate that are inevitably superior. For the Scots, there are the single malts.

Subtle variations in water, weather, peat and the distilling process itself lend each single malt its singular character.

The Classic Malts are the finest examples of the main malt producing regions. To savour them, one by one, is a rare journey of discovery.

For more information about the Classic Malts, write to Janice Mack, Classic Malts Information, 33 Ellersly Road, Edinburgh, Scotland EH12 6JW.

THE 6 CLASSIC MALTS,
FROM THE 6 CLASSIC REGIONS.

SCOTLAND'S SINGLE MALT WHISKIES

While many Scotch drinkers nominate the popular whisky blends when asked to nominate their favourite spirit, a growing number of connoisseurs are also discovering the delights and quality of Scotland's single malts.

The single malts possess traditional, distinctive tastes and are made only from Scottish spring water, malted barley and yeast. The key to each one's individuality and character comes mainly from the water and peat used in its creation. From the west coast islands to Northern Highlands, single malt whiskies reflect the landscape, traditions and atmosphere of their home distillery.

The single malts from the Lowlands are produced south of an imaginary line drawn across Scotland between Dundee in the east and Greenock in the west.

Glenkinchie 10 year old has the distinction of being the driest and smokiest of the Lowland malts. It has an individual taste with a lightly spicy aroma and clean, well-developed flavour.

`Malts from the Highland region make up the largest category of single malts. They are produced north of the Lowlands and cover the areas of Speyside, Northern Highland and West Highland.

Speyside malts are distinguished by their complex tastes and a restrained smoky tone which combine to make an elegant whisky.

Cragganmore 12 year old shows its distiction in the stylish fragrance of its bouquet and the malty, smoky taste which combines with the more usual Speyside characteristics.

Distilleries from the Northern Highlands lie along a line running north from the Monadliath Mountains to Inverness. The malts are fuller in body and have greater individuality than most malts to the south and south east.

At Dalwhinnie Distillery in the Highlands, the locals believe the clarity and purity of the spring water gives this whisky a unique softness. Dalwhinnie has a pleasing heather-honey flavour with a light peaty taste.

The West Highland region embraces a tiny grouping of distilleries on the western coast of the Scottish mainland. A major town in the West Highlands is Oban and its single malt whisky has a good body and round, richness of flavour. Its long maturation period gives it great, soft mellowness and a long smoky finish.

A classic malt from the islands is Talisker, 10 year old malt from the only distillery on the Isle of Skye. It's a full-bodied and well-peated whisky which is rich in concentrated flavour and aroma.

The island of Islay lies off the west coast of Scotland and its malts are so distinctive they form a category in their own right. Lagavulin single malt is a classic example of the dramatic character of Islay. It is deeply smoky and peaty. It is the most pungent and powerful of all Scotch malts reflecting the wind-swept, salt-laden coasts of Islay.

Each malt is unique. It may have the broad characteristics of the region in which it is found but has its own distinct taste and personality. Try some yourself, you won't be disappointed.

*There is no doubt whatever that a section of
the public, who know what they want,
really prefer blends to self-whiskies, and a
still larger section, who know nothing about
the merits of whiskies, have, by this time,
been schooled into drinking blends, and
would not drink a self-whisky..*
- J.A. Nettleton, *The Manufacture of Whisky
and Plain Spirit*, 1913.

*Thomshill and Glenlossie
distilleries, 1925*

ON THIS DAY IN JUL/AUG...

25th July 1796
- Robert Burns dies.

25th July 1901
- Glen Elgin distillery is sold at auction for £4,000 - the building costs had reportedly been
between £13,000 and £14,000.

27th July 1689
- The Battle of Killiecrankie is fought.

28th July 1865
- The last public execution in Britain takes place in Glasgow.

1st August 1914
- Glenkinchie Distillery Co. Ltd goes into liquidation.

THE WATER

In a perfect world, the water which we would add (to our whisky) would come from the distillery's own water supply.

- *The Malt File*, 1993

ELEMENTS SEPARATED BY THE STILLS

During the last century, the older customers of the John's Lane Distillery, Dublin sent two casks to the distillery with their order. One was to be filled with whisky, the other with water from a special tap in the distillery from which flowed the distillery's water supply. In doing this, these customers were uniting once again those elements so rudely separated by the stills.

The water used comes from the Wellglass, a spring in the hills bubbling up for ages past, and mentioned in old records as the "Fairies' looking-glass", from its transparent beauty. Here, it is said, these sprites came from the dells and glades to arrange their tresses and bind on their floral chaplets. This stream, clear and sparkling, is conveyed by a conduit, three miles to the Distillery, where it is used in the manufacture of Limavady whisky, so well known, and which moistens the lips and cheers the hearts of many an "Exile of Erin" in distant Colonies of the Empire.

- Alfred Barnard, *The Whisky Distilleries of the United Kingdom*, 1887.

The water used at Bowmore Distillery comes from the Laggan River, and is conducted by a lade, or water course, nine miles in length, said to be the longest to any distillery in Scotland, though as the crow flies, the distance is not more than five miles, though the engineering difficulties met with were so great, owing to want of fall, that a very tortuous course had to be made.

Much I've heard about the Rhine,

With vineyards gay and castles stately;

But those who think I care for wine

Or lofty towers mistake me greatly:

A thousand times more dear to me

Is whiskey by the silvery Lee.

- Anon

From Tarlogie Springs the water fills a mill pond. Gordon Smart, Glenmorangie distillery manager (1921-1970) inspects the lower dam

*It is a remarkable tribute to John Knox's
ethics that, in a country where enough
whisky has been distilled and drunk during
the four centuries of Presbyterianism to
flavour every loch in Scotland, natives who
take one dram of it at a public festivity like
the Glenbogle Gathering should still be able
to romanticize the little indulgence with the
flavour of mortal sin.*
  - Compton Mackenzie, *The Monarch of
the Glen,* **1941**

Coal fired stills at Glen Grant

ON THIS DAY IN AUGUST...

3rd August 1984
- Glen Grant reverts to coal-fired stills.

4th August 1987
- Ronald Pederson from Albany, New York State, becomes the 1,000,000th visitor to Glenfiddich.

8th August 1978
- The Glenlivet distillery's Reception and Exhibition Centre is officially opened by Robin MacLellan, chairman of the Scottish Tourist Board.

9th August 1935
- James Buchanan (later Lord Woolavington) dies.

11th August 1980
- Queen Elizabeth visits Port Ellen Maltings, and a commemorative bottling from Port Ellen distillery is produced. The distillery is now closed, but the maltings, following a forward-looking concordat entered into by the various distillers in the islands of western Scotland, now produces malted barley for all the distilleries.

EFFLUENT DISPOSALS

Whisky is a very organic product and therefore "green" in modern parlance. Before the industry really knew where it was going, there were problems, particularly around Speyside, of pollution of the rivers. Many methods were tried to dispose of the residues from the distilling process, before it became generally known that these waste products could be used as animal fodder.

The "new" town of Brora was created when the Duke of Sutherland cleared his tenants out of the glens. Brora was the site of a coalfield, whose coal was used to power the distillery which was established in 1819 to make use of excess barley production. The waste products from distilling fed pigs, whose manure was used to fertilise the fields of barley which supplied the distillery's needs.

When Alfred Barnard visited the Glen Kinchie (sic) Distillery at Pencaitland in 1887, he saw:

"...what we had seen nowhere else, - after the spirit is extracted from the wash, there is a very large residue known as dreg, which in towns is very largely used for cattle-feeding purposes but in remote districts is practically useless, and requires to be disposed of in some way; it cannot be emptied into the stream, for the riparian owners would object... it is used by the neighbouring farmer to irrigate his fields, and he is highly pleased with the result.

Barnard also records some lines later, "... we were much struck with the absolute cleanliness which prevailed."

THE DESTRUCTOR

The latest method to come under our notice is a process of burning up the liquid refuse by the waste heat from the still fires as it passes from the flue to the chimney stalk. For this purpose, a destructor was, after several experiments, erected at Longmorn Distillery and has now been in use for several months. The experience already obtained has been very satisfactory and a few notes on the quantity of this liquor used up may be interesting to some of our readers. The destructor referred to is capable of disposing of about three-fourths of the weekly liquid bye products, using the waste heat from the stills only. In any other distillery where the waste heat from the boilers and coppers can be passed through the destructor along with the still fires, the whole of the bye products could very easily be used up. One great advantage of this contrivance is its simplicity in working and economy in labour.

- *The Northern Scot*, 24th January, 1903.

My freens, ye would all like to go to heaven, but what kind of heaven would ye all like to go to? Ye would just like the Cromarty Firth to be bilin' watter, and the Black Isle to be loaf sugar, and the Beauly rinnin' whusky; and ye would just brew and drink and drink and brew to all eternity

- A highland minister preaching to a Banffshire congregation in the 19th century.

Mashing at Benrinnes 1959

*It gives men courage and ambition and the
nerve for anything. It has the colour of gold,
is clear as a glass and shines after dark as if
the sunshine were still in it.*
                    - O. Henry, The Last Blend.

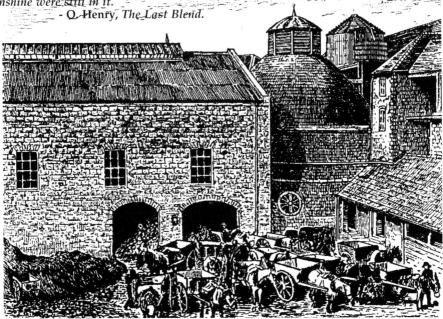

*Farmer's carts at
Monasterevan distillery*

ON THIS DAY IN AUGUST...

15th August 1777
- Sir Walter Scott is born.

16th August 1849
- James Buchanan (later Lord Woolavington) is born.

16th August 1941
- Banff distillery is bombed by a lone German aircraft. Number 12 warehouse is hit, catches fire and burns to the ground. Casks explode and cause others to fly through the air. "...thousands of gallons were lost... even farm animals grazing in the neighbourhood became visibly intoxicated." Cattle cannot be milked because they cannot be got to their feet.

17th August 1822
- George IV lands at Leith for the first ceremonial visit to Scotland by an English monarch. The king toasts the health of Sir Walter Scott, who has organised the ceremonial, in whisky.

19th August 1745
- "Bonnie Prince Charlie" raises his standard at Glenfinnan.

Formerly every event was made an occasion for drinking. If it was raining, it was "we'll have a dram to keep out the wet"; if it was cold, "we'll have a dram to keep out the cold; and if it was a fine day, why then "we'll drink its health".

> - J.A. Macculloch, *The Misty Isle of Skye*, 1905.

A TROUBLESOME DILEMMA

"It would appear at the first blush to be a far cry from the war in the Near East to the distillation of whisky in the Scottish highlands, but nevertheless it has placed Scottish malt whisky distillers on the horns of a very troublesome dilemma. As a result of the feared interruption of barley supplies from the Black Sea and other ports the price of distilling barley has advanced sharply, and, as the season's very inclement conditions have meant that the home crop was anything but superabundant, distillers are faced with the possibility of having to pay for their raw material a price which will add from 4d. to 8d. per gallon to their productive costs according to the locality of their distillery. In the case of the Campbeltown distillers who are more favourably situated for the cheap importation of foreign barley, the addition to productive costs is put at least 4d per gallon."

> - *The Glasgow Herald*, 12th October, 1911.

POOR HARVESTS

A series of poor harvests, due to an extremely cold and wet period for a number of years, hit Scotland in the late 18th and early 19th centuries. By 1800, illicit production had risen to become almost a menace and to the detriment of the health of the populace. James Traill, sheriff of Caithness & Sutherland, wrote in 1783 after a harvest which had been an absolute and total failure:

"The condition of all the north part of Scotland is truly lamentable. In Sutherland and Ross shires, many people have already perished for want of food. This county is not many stages removed from a similar disaster and in Orkney they are nigher to it."

During this time illicit production continued to consume much needed barley supplies. At times such as this landowners were asked to help the Excise eliminate the illicit trade. Angus Mackintosh, who owned an estate near Inverness wrote in 1813:

"I have... suppressed illicit distillation in a very extensive Highland district, my own property. I will never sit on the bench as a Justice of the Peace at an Excise Court where I have not the alternative of either acquitting a miserable half-fed, half-naked wretch or making the penalty less than £20."

For men of sense must own it is better,
To live on malt than to starve on water.

> - Alfred Barnard.

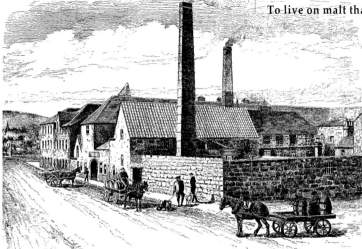

Lochruan distillery

*I do not usually give the mixture of my
whiskies, but may mention that the best is
made in Pitlochry.*
                    - Arthur Bell, Circa 1870.

ON THIS DAY IN AUGUST...

*Tapping the barrels at
Glen Grant*

20th August 1877
- The River Leven bursts its banks. Cameronbridge distillery is flooded - the boiler fires are drowned and casks are washed away.

23rd August 1894
- A.G. Johnstone, the distiller at Glenisla is charged with a breach of the Spirit Act - sending out five and nine-tenths gallons of whisky without a permit. He is fined £5.

25th August 1894
- The first picnic is held by the distillery workers from the distilleries around Dufftown.

26th August 1864
- John Grant, co-founder of Glen Grant, dies.

A PAWKY WAY

An old farmer in the Stirling district, noted for his ready wit and fondness for a dram, was on one occasion visiting another farmer in the district. The host saw that his guest had already been on friendly terms with "John Barleycorn", and had already imbibed sufficient, if not too much mountain dew. Accordingly, after giving his guest one glass, and that a small one, he replaced the bottle in the cupboard.

Conversation on all things interesting to farmers was engaged in, and the time passed pleasantly enough. By-and-bye, however, the guest thought another round of whisky was due and waited patiently for the re-appearance of the bottle, but no bottle was forthcoming. At last wearied out and thirsty, he exclaimed in the pawky way for which he was noted, "God, a man wad soon get sober in this hoose!"

Beneath this stane lies Saummy Noddy;
He was unco fond o' toddy,
But noo the worms ha'e got his body
    -Sae criest and shrunk.
Gin they're din feeding aff Puir Croddy
They'll a' be drunk.

                - Verse on a tombstone in an
                    old churchyard.

John Grant of Glenfiddich & Balvenie, in an open letter to the government in May, 1909, protesting against the proposed increases in the Excise duties, said:

"... if the increased duty is confirmed, it will very adversely affect farming, banking, railways and many other allied and dependent industries in the North of Scotland. To produce the barley required for the North of Scotland (that area north of Perth), 100,000 acres of land are annually under crop."

He went on to say that there was production of 7,000,000 gallons by the 96 northern distilleries in 1906 and that, in the same year, there were 45,000,000 gallons maturing in the north of Scotland.

Worm tubs at
Balvenie distillery

The Highlanders... regale themselves with whisky... They find it an excellent preservation against the winter cold... it is given with great success to the infants... in the confluent smallpox.
  - Tobias Smollett, *Humphrey Clinker,* **1771.**

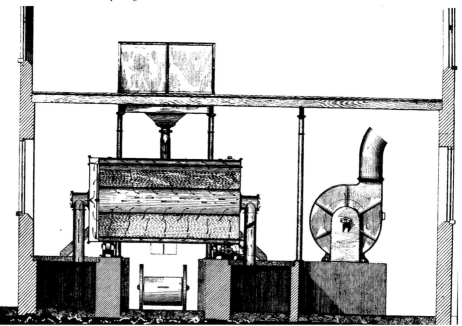

ON THIS DAY IN AUG/SEP...   *Pneumatic malting installation*

31st August 1897
- A letter is published in the Northern Scot blaming distilleries "almost entirely" for "the filthy and abominable state of the bottom of the river" (the Spey). The letter is signed "Stand Fast".

3rd September 1650
- Battle of Dunbar.

4th September 1881
- Fire spreads from a burning haystack to Benrinnes and destroys the distillery's spirit store and the farm's byres and threshing mill.

6th September 1933
- The Old Bushmills Distillery Co. Ltd buys the Coleraine distillery.

9th September 1513
- Battle of Flodden Field.

I received my education in them (malt whiskies) by accident. Walking into a strange pub on the Yorkshire coast I found, beyond the smell of stewing cabbage and dying aspidistras, a little bar at the end where the Proprietress's husband had staked his claim for recognition by amassing a collection of rare and beautiful malt whiskies. The bedroom I booked was completely wasted. Two days later I walked out with an overdraft, a whisky education beyond compare, and the apparent ability to levitate at will.

- Ronnie Corbett, *The Doncella Book of Pubmanship.*

A SPIRIT WORTH DRINKING

French Brandy is, as an article of general consumption, hopelessly discredited, the phylloxera and other diseases of the vine have destroyed the material for the production of a spirit which will suit the ordinary purse. Rum, for some occult reason, nobody that is anybody drinks, except for the medicinal treatment of a cold. Gin, with all its many merits, fails to gain new drinkers, while the old consumers seem to be dying out. The opportunity for Whisky is, therefore, overwhelming. What will it do with it?

England is the market in which both Irish and Scotch Distillers are contending for the pre-eminence; while Caledonia drinks her own Whisky, Hibernia prefers her own make, so that the Saxon taste is the pivot upon which, in these days hangs the prosperity of the Distilling Trade of either nation. To this we have to add the by no means unimportant weight of our Colonial taste, and the fact that wherever on the face of the civilised world Englishmen do congregate, a "good tap" of Whisky is to be found to be irresistible to the British, and a source of profit to "mine host" who has had the luck to secure for his customers something worth their drinking.

- Alfred Barnard, *The Whisky Distilleries of the United Kingdom*, 1887.

"I've had 18 straight whiskies. I think it is a record."

- Dylan Thomas

A NECESSARY EDUCATION

In order that their staffs can converse knowledgeably with their customers, retailers, be they a bottle shop or a bar, have found it necessary, and profitable, to educate their employees on the subject of "Whisky".

The St. Andrews Old Course Hotel, for example, has a "Malt Club" list where they offer, at the time of writing, a choice of 103 single malts, two single grains and a number of blends. I stood in Luvian's Bottle Shop in Cupar, Scotland last summer and counted 383 different single malts, plus a range of blended whiskies. Robertson's of Pitlochry offer a listed 170 whiskies, as well as a similar number unlisted.

These are but three outlets. The education necessary to service such selections is considerable, but whisky, as a subject, engenders considerable, and fiery, passions and the education is thus undertaken willingly.

O, life is a journey we a' hae to gang,
And care is a burden we carry alang -
Though heavy be oor burden, and poverty oor lot,
We are happy wi' oor freens o'er a wee drappie o't.

- Old Scots drinking song.

Death pours a glass (detail)

HIGHLAND PARK

SINGLE MALT SCOTCH WHISKY

ORKNEY ◈ ISLANDS

AGED **12** YEARS

Off the northern-most coast of Scotland lie the green and fertile Islands of Orkney. The majestic waves of the Atlantic Ocean crash onto the cliffs of the western seaboard. The more sheltered inlying islands are surrounded by clear blue seas, rich with fish and many wild birds.

In these remote and beautiful islands, history confronts you everywhere you look, from the 5,000 year old stone ruins of Skara Brae to the ancient stone burial chambers of Maes Howe and Midhowe.

As one might expect in such a place, tradition is important, and nowhere more so than in the world's most northerly Scotch Whisky distillery, Highland Park.

centuries and which impart a rooty, heathery quality to the whisky. Only a carefully measured amount is used to fire the kiln for each malting.

The whisky is then aged for at least twelve years in oak casks. During this time, the fiery spirit mellows and matures. It is a slow, gentle process ensuring that the classic malt has reached perfection.

In his *Malt Whisky Companion*, expert Michael Jackson describes Highland Park as "the greatest all-rounder in the world of malt whisky."

The distillery was founded in 1798 allegedly on the site of a famous whisky smuggler's bothy. The smuggler in question, Magnus Eunson, was also an Elder of the Church, which meant he could hide his illicit whisky under the pulpit where the Excise men were unlikely to find it.

Many believe that the unique character of Highland Park 12 Year Old Single Malt Whisky comes from the local peat beds which have absorbed the salt spray of

Tasting Notes:

Colour:	Glowing amber
Nose:	Balanced smokiness, sweetness, heathery, hint of sherry
Body:	Medium, exceptionally smooth
Palate:	Rounded smoky sweetness. Full malt delivery
Finish:	Teasing, heathery, delicious

Isn't it simply the case that the Treasury puts as high a rate of Excise Duty on Scotch Whisky as it can get away with in order to maximise the tax revenue?
  - Lord Peston in the U.K.'s House of Lords, 1st March, 1993.

Lochnagar distillery warehouses, Aberdeen

ON THIS DAY IN SEPTEMBER...

9th September 1859
- Annie, the daughter of James Macgregor, the distiller at Balmenach, is married in a ceremony at the distillery to John Gardner of the Caledonian Bank.

10th September 1832
- The U.K. Treasury issues a warrant in favour of Aeneas Coffey allowing the use of the Coffey continuous still - the patent being granted on 5th February 1831.

11th September 1297
- Battle of Stirling Bridge.

12th September 1845
- Queen Victoria and Prince Albert visit Lochnagar distillery.

13th September 1897
- Glen Moray produces its first brew with a capacity of 1,700 bushels per week.

THE CLASSIC MALTS

The question which I am asked most frequently is: "Which malt whisky is the best?" A question to which there are an innumerable number of answers.

That great Victorian connoisseur of the good life, Professor George Sainsbury believed that the finest whisky was not a single malt, but a vatting of Clynelish, The Glenlivet and Longmorn.

Every single malt is produced to the same, or at least similar quality criteria. They are effectively the best that the distiller can produce. That each whisky tastes different is an "accident of birth", or locality, as each distillery has subtle differences from its neighbour. Each has a unique micro-climate, unique wild yeasts, unique ambient aromas, unique casks, all of which have a bearing on the ultimate product. Just because consumer "A" intensely dislikes the whiskies from distillery "X", does not mean that it can not be the favourite of consumer "B". Like the whiskies, humans also are unique with differing tastes and preferences.

With this in mind, United Distillers, who at that time owned 49 malt whisky distilleries, almost 50% of malt output, wished to promote some of their range. To promote all 49 would cost a great deal of money and their efforts in favour of one would necessarily detract from the efforts on behalf of another. So which one(s)?

Ian Grieve, the master blender was given the task of examining the range available within the group. He led a panel which tasted a selection of whiskies of various ages and at various strengths.

After their deliberations, they came up with a range of six whiskies, each representative of the region from which they originated. All of very fine quality - and all having very different flavours.

Their choice was:

Glenkinchie at 10 years old and 43% vol., a Lowland;

Cragganmore at 12 years old and 40% vol., a Speyside;

Dalwhinnie at 15 years old and 43%vol., a Northern Highland;

Oban at 14 years old and 43%vol., a Western Highland;

Talisker at 10 years old and 45.8% vol., an Island (Skye);

Lagavulin at 16 years old and 43% vol., an Island (Islay).

United Distillers then found a fitting name for their range, **The Classic Malts**.

Big-headed, or ostentatious? No, because, by definition, each of these whiskies displays the characters of the region of its birth and is therefore a classic in its own right.

Cragganmore distillery

There is good whisky, there is whisky which is not so good, but there is no bad whisky.
   - Dr. Philip Schidrowitz in a lecture to the Institute of Brewing, Glasgow, 15th January, 1907.

Whyte and Mackay's master blender, Richard Paterson, nosing casks in the warehouse

ON THIS DAY IN SEPTEMBER...

14th September 1895
- An announcement is made that a new distillery is to be erected at Pittyvaich, close to the River Dullan - to be named Glenrinnes-Glenlivet and to be owned by Provost Symon of Dufftown.

15th September 1506
- King James IV's treasurer records the purchase of Aqua Vitae in the Exchequer's Rolls.

16th September 1986
- Strathisla celebrates its 200th anniversary.

18th September 1895
- The Banffshire Advertiser announces the plans for Coleburn distillery, which will use the same water supply as Longmorn and Linkwood.

19th September 1970
- Pittyvaich distillery begins production.

NO OAK CASKS

The European Community issued a draft Directive on Hygiene and Foodstuffs during 1992. Among other things, this implied that Scotch Whisky could no longer be aged in oak casks, but would have to be matured in stainless steel, plastic or glass. The E.C.'s food hygienists said that wood, even ancient oak, is unhygienic because it harbours bacteria.

Alan Rutherford, President of the Malt Distillers' Association said that this was:

"Another case where the legislators in Europe have drafted measures with laudable goals, but haven't thought them through. Never has there been a known case of bacterial poisoning from whisky drinking. We don't know of any pathogenic organisms that can live in 40 degrees alcohol."

The Scottish Office at the time confirmed that Scotch Whisky was within the terms of the Directive, but the Scotch Whisky Association soon quelled the public's fears by pointing out that Scotch Whisky production was already covered by E.C. legislation and that this new draft Directive did not apply to Scotch.

The Spirit Act, 1880, held that a distiller was not entitled to a licence unless the distillery was situated within a quarter of a mile of a market town. But a licence could be granted for a distillery outside this radius if the distiller provided "suitable lodgings for the surveying officers." For such lodgings he must not charge more than £15 a year as rent. "These lodgings must be kept in proper repair."

In addition the distiller had to supply lights, ladders and "safety in the discharge of their duties" for the customs officers surveying the distillery.

The distiller had to give the customs officer a minimum of 4 hours notice for any procedure to begin. If he wished to "alter, move, or erect any vessel, utensil or pipe" he had to give 2 days notice.

The distiller was not allowed to deal in or retail wine at the distillery, nor was he allowed to be a "retailer of spirits" within two miles of his distillery.

DISTILLERY OFFICER'S HOUSE AS APPROVED BY H.M. OFFICE OF WORKS. West Elevation. *(By kind permission of H.M.O.W.)*

*One regulation which I think absolutely
necessary and that is to prohibit totally the
Erection of high Walls or other Buildings
about Distilleries, or the keeping of large
Dogs, by which the Officers are prevented
from entering the Works, but at the Hazard
of losing their Lives, or being much hurt.*
**- John Maitland, General Surveyor of Excise
in Scotland, 1798.**

ON THIS DAY IN SEPTEMBER...   *Barley on the malting floor*

21st September 1891
- Andrew Carnegie orders a "9 or 10 gallon cask" from Dewars to be sent to U.S. President Benjamin Harrison.

22nd September 1887
- W. & A. Gilbey buy Glenspey distillery.

23rd September 1924
- Lord Mackie of White Horse dies.

27th September 1905
- The A.G.M. of Benrinnes-Glenlivet Distillery Co. Ltd. shows a profit increase and growth despite "the still depressed state of the whisky market".

28th September 1830
- The distillery utensils and a lease for 12 years of Milton distillery are sold by public roup.

THE SURVIVOR

An old pensioner of the 42nd. (one of the old Highland Regiments) and a good judge of "Glenlivat" was brought before a bailie (the judge in a Scottish court which deals with small misdemeanours) of a charge of over-indulgence in his favourite beverage.

It was not, by any means his first offence, and he trotted out his usual plea that he was one of the last survivors of the battle of Waterloo. To this the bailie replied, "Weel, Sandy, I'll let ye aff this time; but mind ye - and it's as sure as death - if ye come here again, I'll clap ye in jail, though ye were the last survivor o' the battle o' Bannockburn!"

- Dean Ramsay, *Reminiscences of Scottish Life and Character*, 1899.

I t is not lawful to distil spirit from any other material than malt, corn or grain, or any mixture thereof.

- Act 4 Geo. IV c.94. s.17, 1823.

THE MALT BARNS

In 1510, the Burgh Records of Edinburgh state that three acres of the Burgh Muir (now the Meadows) were let to build thereon Malt Barns, and that servants were to be hired for the making of malt from 30th April to Michaelmas, and that failing to do that the lessees were to pay a £40 fine and a penalty of £5 per acre.

Till 1847, the legal materials were -

Grain, malted and unmalted   Potatoes

Sugar (duty-paid)   Mangel-wurzel

But as only grain, malted and unmalted, was allowed to be used in combination, and as Customs duty was payable on the sugar used, practically only grain, malted and unmalted, was used.

- Report of the Inland Revenue Commissioners, 1870.

In 1958 a fire destroyed Glenmorangie's malt kiln. It was rebuilt exactly as before

The GLENLIVET ®

THE STORY OF THE GLENLIVET

The Glenlivet Distillery produces arguably the most historic and famous malt whisky in Scotland and the one to which whisky experts give pride of place. Its heritage goes back over 200 years and spans seven generations of distillers from the Smith family. From its early days The Glenlivet has set many of the standards by which lesser whiskies are judged.

CASTLES THREE

"Glenlivet", the old rhyme runs, "has it castles three, Drumin, Blairfindy and Deskie; And also one distillery more famous than the castles three." The reputation of The Glenlivet Malt Whisky had spread so rapidly that King George IV, during a visit to Scotland in 1822, demanded The Glenlivet and declared he would drink no other.

ILLICIT STILLS

In the early nineteenth century there were said to be 200 illicit stills in the area, so ideal a place was it for the making of whisky. When George Smith took out his licence, in accordance with the Excise Act of 1823, he became the first farmer in the district to operate inside the law. Many of his neighbours regarded his defection from their smuggling ranks as a threat to their own survival. In sympathy with his predicament Smith was presented with a a handsome pair of matching hair trigger pistols by the Laird of Aberlour to defend himself against local wrath.

STUNNINGLY BEAUTIFUL

The Glenlivet is distilled in the Spey Valley, in the heart of the Scottish Highlands. Throughout the seasons - from rugged winters to gentle summers - the scenery at The Glenlivet Distillery is stunningly beautiful. No district in Scotland is more suitable for distilling whisky than the isolated, peaceful glen in which The Glenlivet Distillery lies. It is as if Nature has conspired to provide the perfect conditions.

The Glenlivet Distillery uses water from a local spring, known as Josie's Well, and its four wash stills and four spirit stills produce a malt whose lightness and delicacy reflect generations of skill and craftsmanship.

QUINTESSENTIAL

The Glenlivet Pure Single Malt Scotch Whisky, aged 12 years, is the quintessential Speyside malt whisky. Owned by Seagram since 1978, it is today one of the top-selling brands of malt whisky and appreciated by connoisseurs the world over.

A smuggler is a person who, though no doubt highly blameable for violating the laws of his country, is frequently incapable of violating those of natural justice, and would have been in every respect an excellent citizen had not the laws of his country made that a crime which Nature never meant it to be.

- Adam Smith

ON THIS DAY IN SEP/OCT...

Aberlour floor malting

29th September 1973
- Braes of Glenlivet distillery goes into production.

30th September 1881
- Mr. W. Edwards entertains his employees and their friends to a ball at Benrinnes distillery "in recognition of the services of the villagers of Aberlour and others in assisting to extinguish the fire which recently occurred".

1st October 1784
- The Wash Act comes into effect.

1st October 1814
- Stills of less than 2,000 gallons in the Lowlands and less than 500 gallons in the Highlands are outlawed.

In his dictionary, Dr. Johnson described the word "Excise" as: "a hateful tax levied upon commodities and adjudged not by the common judges of property but by wretches hired by them to whom the Excise is paid".

A PERMANENT IMPOSITION

During the past 12 years the conditions prevailing in the industry have been in some respects well nigh revolutionised. In those days none dreamt of an Excise duty of 14s. 9d. per proof gallon on home made spirits in normal times. As a war tax, it was conceivable, but it was generally accepted that as a permanent imposition 10s. 6d. per gallon was the most the industry could stand.

- *The Glasgow Herald*, 3rd August, 1911.

PROPORTIONATELY AUGMENTED

The present duty is levied, in three different ways, and consists (per gallon) of £108 annually, on the content of the still; of 11s. 2d. on the wash, in working, and of 1s. on the spirit, when manufactured.

By the lowest estimate, the still is drawn of 96 times a day, during 200 days in the year; and 48 times, during 100; in the working, 96 gallons wash produce 19 gallons spirit; therefore each gallon content may be said to afford 4,750, which, at 108s., is about 51s. 2d. per gallon; add to this 71s. 2d. for the wash duty, and 1s. for the spirit duty, the whole amounts to 2s. 1d.

About ten years ago, there was only an annual tax of £1. 10s. per gallon on the content, which was raised successively to £9, £18, £27, £54 and £108. When it was at £9, a meeting was held at Edinburgh, by the gentlemen deputed on the part of the distillers, and of the corn growers, from all parts of Scotland, at which it was generally agreed that the manufacture could bear no higher imposition; yet since the very great increase, the profit, both to the distillers and to the Revenue, has been more than proportionably augmented. A single manufacturer is said to have realised £160,000, in a very few years: and the produce of the customs of Scotland (of which this forms the chief part), from July 1798 to July 1799 amounted to £260,000.

- John Stoddart, Llb. in *Remarks on Local Scenery & Manners.*

Doctor Johnson

The general tendency of the evidence on these matters was to show that any special evil effects were rather to be attributed to the excessive quantity consumed than to any special deleterious substance.
  - Royal Commission on Whisky and Other Potable Spirits, 1909.

Benrinnes distillery
headed paper

ON THIS DAY IN OCTOBER...

2nd October 1897
- Mr. McGregor, fishery inspector, expresses himself satisfied that the settling ponds at Benrinnes removed the pollution from the distillery's outflow and "that the flow from Benrinnes distillery could do no harm to fish life".

3rd October 1896
- A tramway connecting Glenlossie distillery with the railway at Longmorn station is formally opened.

13th October 1893
- The Elgin Courant reports that "the proprietor of Longmorn (the estate) has given off a feu for the purpose of erecting a distillery".

The Rev. Mr. John Downie of Urray in the presbytery of Dingwall said in the Statistical Account of 1793:

"The worst effect of the great plenty of spirits is, that dram shops are set up in almost every village for retail, where young and idle people convene and get drunk. The tipling huts are kept by such only as are not able to pay a fine or procure a licence. They are the greatest nuisance in the parish."

THE DANGERS OF LEGISLATION

Let Government then take care how they tamper with a law that works well, and satisfies all parties, the distiller, the consumer, and the Exchequer, and especially, let them beware of fettering the distiller in his processes one iota beyond what is indispensable. The moment you place him under restrictions that deteriorate quality of the spirits, the smuggler resumes his superiority. We wish Mr. Robinson were in reach of our voice, we would remind him of the many horrid blunders made by his predecesors as to the distillery laws, and we would ring in his ears a maxim of his own - LET WELL ALONE.

- *The Inverness Journal*, 25th November 1825, echoing the distillers' reservation about the introduction of legislation imposing the spirit safe.

AN INCONVENIENCE TO THE DISTILLER

The main object of all legal provisions is the protection of the Revenue and its economical collection. They are also designed to prevent complex and irregular methods of working, which would, if permitted, require the attendance of additional officials. The legislation referring to distilleries is indeed based upon centuries of experience. The restrictions increase the cost of production slightly, but, more seriously, they, at times, inconvenience the distiller and prevent new inventions and improvements from being applied.

- J.A. Nettleton, *The Manufacture of Whisky & Plain Spirit*, 1913.

Newly coopered barrels at Craigellachie

Long ago, it was said that if you drink the right amount of Scotch each day, you will find the secret of Eternal Youth. People have been in pursuit ever since.
- **Ian Henderson, manager, Laphroaig distillery.**

Peat used to arrive at Glenmorangie by "puffers" which beached themselves below the distillery, allowing them to be off-loaded at low tide

ON THIS DAY IN OCTOBER...

18th October 1860
- World's first professional golf tournament is played at Prestwick and won by Willie Park.

18th October 1860
- Distilling starts at Glen Cawdor distillery.

20th October 1871
- The Elgin Courant reports that "the great distillery of Inchgower has been erected".

FOCAL POINTS

In many cases distilleries have developed in areas of low population and have become focal centres of the local economy, e.g. Campbeltown towards the end of the 19th century. Apart from providing direct employment for the community, many local trades provide services for the distillery. Although the numbers directly employed are considerably lower than they were previously, in areas of irregular, and seasonal, employment, distilleries are very important.

Bowmore Distillery donated a warehouse to the local community which was converted into a swimming pool. The funds required were raised by the village and the distillers donated cash, as well as time and effort in organising events and attracting personalities. A waste-heat re-circulation system is in use at the distillery and the system heats the water for the swimming pool and provides heating for the complex.

The swimming pool and sauna were opened in 1991.

When Alfred Barnard visited Bunnahabhain distillery in 1885, he recorded that:

"A Reading Room and School Room have likewise, with praiseworthy liberality, been provided by the Company, and in the latter the children of the workmen receive an elementary education."

RECORDING THE TEMPERATURE

Dalwhinnie distillery is Station 0582 of the Meteorological Office. One of the distillery manager's daily responsibilities is to make a record of maximum and minimum temperatures, the number of hours of sunshine, wind speed and snow depth. He is also ex-officio, a trustee of Dalwhinnie village hall.

In former times the only trade of the place was herring fishing, net making and smuggling.

During the last century and up to seventy years ago the unlawful occupation of distilling Whisky was carried on to the greatest extent, the landed proprietors rather encouraging the practice. Those found smuggling by the Excise Officers were brought before the Court of Justice and fined; but usually the judge was one of the landed proprietors, so the fines were small and many got off free. When legal distilling was first introduced, the Distillers met with a good deal of opposition and resentment from the smugglers, but they managed to live it down, and owing to the quality of the product, the trade developed so rapidly that it has now become the staple article of commerce, and there are no less than twenty-one Distilleries in Campbeltown.

- Alfred Barnard, *The Whisky Distilleries of the United Kingdom*, 1887.

Stillhouse, Nevis distillery

The common belief that whisky improves with age is true. The older I get, the more I like it.
            - Ronnie Corbett, *The Doncella Book of Pubmanship.*

ON THIS DAY IN OCTOBER...

23rd October 1937
- D.C.L. sign the feu contract for Brackla distillery.

24th October 1885
- The North British Distillery Company Ltd. is founded.

28th October 1976
- I.D.V. informs a public meeting at Nethybridge of plans to build a brand new distillery at Garlyne, Nethybridge.

AN ADAPTABLE SPIRIT

Scotch Whisky is an amazingly adaptable spirit. Because of the diversity of flavours, and intensity of flavours, it can be drunk at any time of day, accompany the most delicate, or most spicily flavoured foods.

The Invergordon Distillers Information Service on Scotch Whisky has recently introduced a leaflet entitled "Summer Scotch". Included in this leaflet are a number of recipes for summer cocktails. Trevor Cowan, the master blender at Invergordon was interviewed on Radio Scotland and claimed that his favourite was a Frozen Gael, the recipe for which is detailed below:

FROZEN GAEL

One half Scotch Whisky

One half Baileys Irish Cream

One scoop vanilla ice cream

Half scoop crushed ice

Mix in an electric blender, pour into a large champagne saucer or similar - add a slice of orange.

THE LAPHROAIG COOLER

Some years ago, The Pot Still public house in Glasgow ran a series of Malt of the Month promotions. The publican, John Waterston, had agreed to promote Laphroaig in June. The month turned out to be one of the hottest Junes on record and, as May was running out, the forecast temperatures for June were remarkably high.

The first of June dawned bright, clear - and hot. The whisky had arrived, but John foresaw limited take-up for what is after all a highly flavoured malt. Then in a blinding flash he had an idea.

He sent out for copious quantities of fresh orange juice and ice. A measure of Laphroaig was poured over crushed ice and diluted with fresh orange. The Laphroaig Cooler was born!

FILLETS OF PORK IN A WHISKY AND CREAM SAUCE

1 Fillet of pork

1 Glass of malt (a light Speyside, such as Tamnavulin is ideal, or otherwise a Lowland such as Glenkinchie or Rosebank)

1 Tablespoonful of olive oil

pint single cream

Salt & pepper

Closed.   **FIG.1.**

Open.   **FIG.2.**

Cut the fillet into small pieces and beat out until very thin. Salt and pepper and cook gently for three minutes each side in the olive oil. Remove from the pan and lay to one side. Add the whisky, reduce and add the cream. Return the fillets to the pan. Cover and leave the dish to marinate off the heat until you are ready for it.

*It is of paramount importance that only the
very best materials that can be procured
should be used in the manufacture of whisky.
When these only are used, and when the
whisky has been sufficiently matured in
sherry casks (which are of unpurchaseable
benefit to it), there can be no more
wholesome spirit, and in purity, fragrance
and ease of digestion it is superior to the
finest French brandy.*
                    - William B. Gloag , 1826 - 1896.

ON THIS DAY IN OCTOBER...

*Convalmore group
photograph 1902*

28th October 1976
- Major Douglas MacKessack of Glen Grant, dies.

29th October 1894
- The first spirit is produced at Knockdhu distillery.

29th October 1909
- Fire breaks out at Convalmore distillery. The Malt Barn, Mash House and Tun Room are destroyed by the conflagration. At its height, the flames rise to between 30 and 40 feet high; snow also begins to fall and provides for the fire-fighters and spectators, a never to be forgotten sight.

KING PRAWNS OBAN

1 dozen king prawns
1 medium sized onion
1oz. butter
1 tablespoonful olive oil
1 clove garlic
pinch paprika
Glass of Oban 14 years old Malt

Melt the butter in a heavy-based frying pan. Fry the onions and garlic gently for a few minutes. Add the paprika and prawns. Cover the pan and toss the shellfish over a medium heat until the shells turn reddish-brown. Add the whisky and toss the prawns again. When the sauce starts to bubble, serve immediately.

In olden times it was customary for every traveller to stop at Moulinearn, a place just above the junction of the Tay and Tummel, to refresh himself with a glass of "Athole Brose", a celebrated local compound of whisky and honey. The natives have a high opinion of it, but we must confess a preference for the whisky by itself or with a small addition of the crystal stream from the hills.

- Alfred Barnard, *The Whisky Distilleries of the United Kingdom*, 1887.

A DIVERSE SPIRIT

Few spirits present such diversely different, distinctive tastes, worth sampling in their own right as single malts and single grains or as a blended Scotch whisky. Conservatively for the connoisseur, or in the wackiest way possible for the adventurous explorer, as an aperitif, a digestif, or just as a long thirst quencher with food indoors or out, after an energy-sapping event or a lazy afternoon in the garden, the opportunities are endless and success is guaranteed.

- The Invergordon Distillers Information Service on Scotch Whisky, 1993.

CO_2 refrigerating machine

THE FAMOUS GROUSE
FINEST SCOTCH WHISKY

The Red Grouse, Scotland's national gamebird, a distinctive and noble inhabitant of the magnificent heather-clad mountains and glens of the Scottish Highlands, is a fitting emblem for this renowned whisky.

Introduced in the 1890s, The famous grouse continues to make new friends throughout the world every year. Its overall balance and rich appearance are expressions of its subtlety and difference over other Scotch Whiskies. A smooth, medium peated, well rounded whisky, it has a touch of dryness which allows the complexity of the blend to show through.

The Famous Grouse has truly become the Scotch Whisky against which all others are judged by the discerning Scotch Whisky drinker. The care and skill that goes into making The Famous Grouse the finest of Scotch Whiskies, may be measured by the fact that it is the most popular Scotch Whisky amongst the people who should know about whisky - the Scots themselves.

Today, The Famous Grouse is drunk wherever discerning whisky drinkers are to be found, throughout the world.

To ensure that demand continues to be met, and that the character and quality of the blend are preserved for generations to come, Matthew Gloag & Son Limited plan forward for a minimum of eight years, in order to secure the quality mature malt and grain whiskies required for The Famous Grouse.

For ultimately it is the quality of The Famous Grouse which makes it so special - a quality which has been maintained for close on 100 years - quality which has become the hallmark of the blend... Quality in an age of change.

"A splendid blend with a restrained sweet maltiness and a hint of sherry in its long finish."

-Michael Jackson,
The World Guide to Whisky.

*Like the monks of old, the Highland
Distillers have located themselves "where
every prospect pleases".*
                        - Alfred Barnard.

*Braes of Glenlivet -
a "modern" distillery*

ON THIS DAY IN OCT/NOV...

30th October 1824
- Cameronbridge distillery is licensed.

31st October 1968
- "Balmenach", the railway locomotive belonging to that distillery steams out of the distillery for the last time. It can now be seen in the Strathspey Railway Museum at Boat of Garten.

1st November 1897
- One man is killed and another seriously injured when scaffolding collapses during the building of Imperial distillery.

4th November 1966
- The last delivery of coal is made to Clynelish distillery. One of the reasons for the establishment of Clynelish on the site of Brora was the proximity of a local coalfield. The coal stocks had long since been exhausted and, in 1966, the distillery became oil-fired.

PAID A COMPOSITION

Some of the Officers who Surveyed Distilleries were suspected of being corrupted by the Distillers... One instance of an Endeavour to bribe an Officer, not immediately by the Distiller himself, but by his brother... a very extensive Distillery carried on at Cannonmills (sic), near Edinburgh, by Mr. James Haig. I placed Six Expectants as Watchmen on that Work. One of these Expectants, viz. John Gordon, came up to me one Evening and presented Five Guinea Notes of the Royal Bank of Scotland, which he said he had just got put into his Hand by Mr. Robert Haig, one of Mr. James Haig's Brothers... a Prosecution was ordered in the Exchequer, and I believe Mr. Robert Haig paid a Composition of Fifty Pounds, and Mr. Gordon got the Five Guineas.

- Answers of John Maitland, General Surveyor of Excise in Scotland, to certain Questions submitted to him respecting the Scottish Distillery, 1798.

Some 60 years ago, the postmaster of Kingussie, returning from Aberlour, arrived at Dalnasheugh Inn on a stormy evening, and was promised lodgings for himself and his pony.

He was well attended until a party of half-a-dozen excisemen arrived on their way to make a raid on certain bothies well known to be at work in Badenoch. They were treated to the best the inn could afford, while the postmaster was ordered to the kitchen. He told the servant girl that she had better go to bed, and that he would mount his pony when the moon arose.

When she left the kitchen he pitched the boots of the Excisemen, which were drying at the fire, into a pot of boiling water. He then started for Badenoch, and sent warning to all the bothies he was acquainted with. The officers could not move for want of boots, and by the time they got to Badenoch everything was in order.

- William Harvey, *Scottish Life and Character*, 1899.

DROONED IT!

"I say, Dugald, man," enquired Donald, "have ye ony excisemen in Skye?"

"Er - what kind of thing's that?" asked Donald. "Och! juist wan of thae bodies that goes aboot lookin' for stills o' whusky, and that." "Oo-oo-oo ay!" replied Dugald. "We had wan, but we drooned it."

Cardow group photograph , 1902

*For a bad hangover take the juice of two
quarts of whisky.*
                              - Eddie Condon.

ON THIS DAY IN NOVEMBER...   *Glenlivet - steam lorries, 1924*

6th November 1865
- Duke of Richmond, landlord of Glenlivet, states that "The Glenlivet" distillery is now the
only distillery in the Glenlivet district.

7th November 1849
- William Matheson announces that Glen-Morange (sic) distillery has opened.

10th November 1893
- Notice of sale of Benrinnes distillery for £32,000.

11th November 1839
- James and John Grant are granted entry to the Feu at Rothes where Glen Grant is to be built.

11th November 1892
- A special train leaves Rothes station with 12,000 gallons of whisky from "Messrs. J. & J.
Grant's famous Glengrant distillery."

The writer first tasted whisky during an attempt to climb the Cairngorm Range in the late autumn of 1918. The weather was cold; snow was falling and the fingers were so chilled that the packets of sandwiches remained uneaten - it was impossible to untie the strings.

The guide broke the ice of a burn, took up a little water in a tin cup and laced it with something from a bottle. The delicious concoction (for it is not true that most people dislike whisky when they taste it for the first time) transformed the world. The generous warmth spread to the finger tips and to the frozen toes inside the heavy boots.

One realised that to the Highlander whisky was not a luxury but a necessity, a necessity which has been put, alas! increasingly out of his reach by excessive taxation.

- James Laver, *The House of Haig*, 1958.

THE TEETOTALER

He had a strong impression that there was a close affinity between a flask and a fish! Once, when the author accompanied him to Kingcardine O'Neil, in the early part of April, they each got a fish in the forenoon. On going down the river in the afternoon, they met a brother-angler coming up. The usual enquiries as to sport were made, when Brown told him of our success, at which he seemed surprised, and said he had fished all morning, but had done nothing.

"Are ye aye a teetotaler yet?" said Brown.

"Yes," said the other, "and I intend to remain so."

Brown's reply, in the shape of another query, was brief: "Man, do ye think a fish wad be sic a fool as to come to a man that hadna a flask in his pouch?"

- John MacVine, *Sixty-Three Years Angling*, 1891.

Mural of Aberlour distillery in the manager's office

The skill of the blender lies in orchestrating these numerous and diverse tastes to ensure that the consumer perceives no variation in the taste of his favourite tipple.

> - The Invergordon Distillers Information Service on Scotch Whisky, 1993.

ON THIS DAY IN NOVEMBER... *Knockdhu distillery, 1898*

13th November 1900
- Charles Souter, rat catcher, having already killed between 3 and 4,000 rats at Cragganmore in September, returns to exterminate the plague of rats.

15th November 1852
- Dail-Uaine distillery opens.

16th November 1827
- Malcolm Gillespie is hanged.

17th November 1825
-A meeting of Distillers of the Northern Counties tells the government that the proposed spirit safe "is considered useless and oppressive to the trade".

19th November 1989
- Knockdhu distillery is sold to Inver House Distillers.

Whisky Blending. - At one time the individual makes of the various distilleries were consumed unblended, but during the past forty or fifty years the public taste has changed to lighter spirits in the form of mixtures of malts and grains. The art of whisky blending is by no means easily acquired.

> - Arthur Bourke, editor of *Winecraft - The Encyclopaedia of Wines & Spirits*, **1935.**

Before the passing of this Act (1860), duty-paid spirits only were allowed to be blended in warehouse. The provision was introduced to place the home manufacturer on an equal footing with the foreigner, to give greater facilities for carrying on the trade.

> - *Bateman's Excise Officers' Manual*, 1864.

THE VERNACULAR

The Aberdeen vernacular is quite unique in its way. The natives have an extraordinary habit of pronouncing words beginning with the letter "w" as if it were "f". The Aberdonian is proverbially acute, and well knows how to look to the interests of 'number one'. An elderly client gave the author an account of his first experiences in business amongst them, of which the following is given as nearly verbatim as possible.

'A respectable-looking gentleman came into my shop and asked,

"Fat's the price o' yer fusky the gallon?"

It was long before the duty was advanced, so I said, "I have some very good at ten shillings."

He said, "Can ye let me see a sample o't?"

I put about a wine glassful in a tumbler, thinking he might want some water to it. He looked at it in the glass, smelt it and drank about the half of it.

"Ay," he said, that's verry good! Have ye naething a wee bittie stronger?"

I said I could let him have some unreduced at twelve shillings. He asked for a sample of it. I gave him a similar quantity in another tumbler. He drank the half of it, and liked it better; then said,

"I think they would mak' a good fusky if they were mixed!"

He then poured the contents of the one tumbler into the other, and drank the lot, saying, "That's a great improvement; I'll ca' in and see ye some other day!"'

> - John MacVine, *Sixty-Three Years Angling*, 1891.

A private still in the 19th century

I like the whisky old and the women young.
                    - Errol Flynn.

ON THIS DAY IN NOVEMBER...

Visitor centre at
Glenfarclas distillery

22nd November 1960
- Talisker distillery's stillhouse is destroyed by fire.

24th November 1993
- Christie's Glasgow will hold their now annual whisky auction at their Bath Street premises.

26th November 1855
- Electric light is installed at Benrinnes distillery. The distillery is reported to be mashing 2,620 bushels per week and the make is booked for a year in advance.

29th November 1785
- Duncan Forbes of Ferintosh loses "The Privilege". This is the privilege of distilling free of Excise duty in recognition of his support for the English monarch in 1688 and the fact that Forbes's lands were laid to waste by the Jacobites. This meant that Forbes could sell his Ferintosh whisky at a lower price than any other legal distillery. The Ferintosh brand became the first recognisable "brand" of whisky. The "Privilege" was abused and subsequently taken away. Robert Burns wrote:

> Thee Ferintosh! O sadly lost!
>
> Scotland lament frae coast to coast!
>
> Now colic grips and barkin' hoast
>
> May kill us a';
>
> For loyal Forbes chartered boast
>
> Is ta'en awa!

MOONEY'S WIFE

At Mabrista, a secluded nook near Brusna Distillery, Kilbeggan in Eire, formerly lived one "Mooney", who carried on his nefarious practices under the very nose of the revenue people. On one occasion, a raid was about to be made upon him; Mooney, seeing in the distance the officers coming, called out to his wife to hide the three kegs of whisky in the garret.

The ready-witted woman placed them in the middle of the floor, and then brought up her feather bed, which she ripped open, and completely covered the kegs. After searching all the rest of the house, the captain of the party entered the garret, and seeing nothing there but a huge heap of feathers, called to his men that there was nothing in the damned old cockloft but feathers, and it was useless to spoil their clothes by removing them.

A capital story is told of an old woman who resided near Hazelburn. She was of a rather doubtful character and was charged before the Sheriff with smuggling. The charge being held proven, it fell to his lordship to pronounce sentence. When about to do so he thus addressed the culprit,

"I daresay my poor woman it is not often that you have been guilty of this fault."

"Deed no Sheriff," she readily replied, "I hae nae made a drap since yon wee keg I sent to yersel."

BEGINNING THE DAY

"Decent gentlewomen began the day with a dram. In our house, the bottle of whisky with its accompaniment of a silver salver full of small glasses, was placed on the side-table with cold meat every morning. In the pantry a bottle of whisky was the allowance per day, with bread and cheese in any required quantity, for such messengers or visitors whose errands sent them in that direction. The very poorest cottages could offer whisky, all the men engaged in the wood manufacture drank it in goblets three times a day, yet except at a merry-making we never saw anyone tipsy."

- Elizabeth Grant of Rothiemurchus, *Memoirs of a Highland Lady*, 1845-1867.

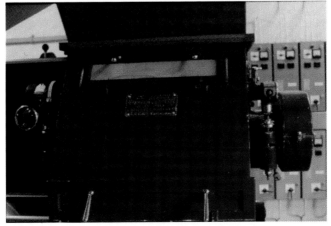

Porteous mill

Time for a Scotch - I don't really care!
                    - Keith Floyd.

ON THIS DAY IN NOV/DEC...   *Bowmore distillery*

30th November 1851
- Mrs. Grant (of Glen Grant) cuts the first sod for the railway line into the village of Rothes.

1st December 1785
- T. Simpson announces that "spirit will be ready about the 10th instant" at the licensed distillery in Old Meldrum (Glen Garioch).

2nd December 1880
- 4,000 gallons of whisky, belonging to the executors of the late James Kay of Glenburgie distillery are advertised for sale at "a Moderate Price".

2nd December 1902
- Glendullan receives its Royal Appointment.

3rd December 1892
- Highland Distillers purchases Glenglassaugh distillery.

In whisky terms, many measures are somewhat indeterminate in exact quantity. The old standard "pub" measures of anything from one sixth (a rather niggardly size) to a quarter gill (as in some of Scotland's more enlightened hostelries) will be replaced, in 1994, by either a 25ml. or a 50 ml. measure. A "gill" is a measure equal to one fourth of a pint.

Many public houses have on display a series of old pewter measures which can include one sixth, one fifth, one quarter, one half, one gill and if the collection is very old, a Scots gill.

Historically, the Scots pint was larger than its English counterpart, the Scots variety being equal to one third of an imperial gallon, so that a Scots gill was a good measure.

A "dram" in a public house can be any one of the measures listed above. A "dram" in a private home, however, can be anything from a splash which merely dampens the bottom of the glass to great tumblerfuls. I have heard one woman complaining that "They're making whisky bottles much smaller these days." When asked why she thought this, her reply was, "I only get six drams from a bottle nowadays."

A "glass" or "gless" is normally accepted to be a double measure, or a large dram in a private house. Mrs. Macdonald's remark about the size of a bottle would mean three glasses from her bottle!

THE CORDIAL DRAM

All that is contended for on behalf of the Highlanders is that he shall have liberty on moderate terms suited to the poverty of his circumstances to convert the growth of his own soil through his personal industry to the necessary beverage of his wholesome spirit, ...taken as a cordial dram to brace sometimes the bleak piercing winds of the North.

- John Grant of Balnagown, 1798.

Frien'ship maks us a mair happy,
Frien'ship gies us a' delight;
Frien'ship consecrates the drappie,
Frien'ship brings us here to-night.

Like all people who have known hard times, light-heartedness seemed to her too irrational and inconsequent to be indulged in except as a reckless dram now and then.

- Thomas Hardy, *The Mayor of Casterbridge*, 1886.

Mixing the punch

SINGLE ISLAY MALT
SCOTCH WHISKY

LAPHROAIG:
AS UNIQUE AS THE ISLAND ITSELF...

Some say it's the pure local water, softened by hard granite rocks. Others remark on the salty sea air, laden with the iodine aroma of seaweed. Yet others point to the swirling smoke of a peat-fuelled fire, used to dry barley. But in truth, it's a mix of all these things, and more besides, which makes Laphroaig- the famous whisky from the Island of Islay - so distinctive.

It was in 1815, the year of Wellington's triumph at Waterloo, that brothers Donald and Alec Johnston established the Laphroaig Distillery. Laphroaig is a Gaelic word which means "the beautiful hollow by the broad bay" and there is no better description for the hauntingly evocative environment which surrounds the distillery.

As the most southerly of Scotland's mystical Western Isles, Islay meets the full fury of the Atlantic's notorious South Westerly storms. Windblown and often shrouded in mist, it's a wild place indeed. Yet the rugged climate is softened by the waiting Gulf Stream, and when the sun shines there are few beaches more enchanting than the white strands which gird this magical Gaelic island. It's fitting, then, that Laphroaig should be every bit as mystical and suited to changing moods as the island itself.

Understanding how Laphroaig achieves its distinctive character is no easy task. What is certain is that the stillmen are justly proud of the traditional malting process which is still used to this day at Laphroaig.

Malt whisky production isn't just a business here, it's an art form, created from all the gifts which the four elements of air, water, earth and fire can bestow.

The mashing and fermentation takes place in large vats, with the cloudy, fermented brew of malt, water and yeast then being distilled in beautiful swan-necked copper stills to produce a clear and fragrant liquid.

After a second distillation, the whisky is transferred to oak casks in which it slowly matures, for at least 10 years, to acquire from the wood its deep, golden glow and matchless rich, mellow flavour.

Laphroaig - pronounced "lafroyg" is certainly easier to drink than it is to say! Though most prefer to drink Laphroaig straight or with the simple addition of water - for real devotees this should ideally be the same water from which the whisky is made - others will add a few cubes of ice.

Just one sip is enough to distinguish the richly smoky, seaweedy and yet fully peated taste for which Laphroaig is renowned the world over. It comes as no surprise that Laphroaig has been hailed by many connoisseurs as the rightful King of Single Malt Whiskies.

The distillery is open from September to the end of June. Tours available by appointment only. Contact the Laphroaig Distillery, Port Ellen, Isle of Islay, Argyll PA427DU Telephone: 0496 2418

THE GLENDRONACH TRADITIONAL
- A WHISKY FOR WHICH TIME STANDS STILL

The GLENDRONACH
TRADITIONAL
Single Highland Malt Scotch Whisky

It's rare to find a malt whisky that draws together the richness of sherry and the zest and freshness of seasoned oak, but The Glendronach Traditional, a malt from the heart of the Scottish Highlands, has found that perfect combination.

The Glendronach or "Valley of the Brambles", as it was known in Gaelic, aptly describes the beautiful setting of the distillery which nestles by the Dronac burn deep in the Valley of Forgue, near Huntly in Aberdeenshire.

The Traditional is still made with the same care and attention since the distillery was legally licensed to James Allardes many years ago in 1826. Distilled on the very same spot, The Glendronach is now one of the oldest working distilleries in Scotland. The very name "Traditional" conjures up a vivid image of the time-honoured craftsmanship of which the workers at the distillery are justly proud.

Every aspect of the malt whisky process from malting to maturation is in the hands of the distillery itself - and this hasn't changed for over 160 years!

There aren't many distilleries which still malt their own barley, but this is just one example of the attention to detail which sets The Glendronach apart from other malts. In long, low-ceilinged rooms, the germinating grain, soaked and brought to life by spring water, is spread in a soft carpet on the malting floors. There it was turned by hand with traditional wooden shovels known

as shiels and ploughed with the rakes in the way it always has been done.

Peat and fine steam coal provide the gentle warmth in the kiln to dry the barley and halt germination, while the peat imparts a unique flavour to the malt as it dries so that it becomes crisp and aromatic. Traditional wooden washbacks of Oregon pine are used for fermentation. When the whisky is ready for its first distillation, it is placed in copper stills which have shapes and dimensions which can only be found at this distillery. The unique shape of each still has a marked effect on the final character of the whisky. Consistency is guaranteed when the stills are replaced because each new still is made as an exact replica of the old.

Seasoned oak wood casks and those which have previously held sherry are carefully chosen for the maturation of The Glendronach Traditional. Both woods impart a subtle flavour to the whisky which helps to bring out the richly distinctive taste of The Glendronach. Surrounded by the clear, fresh air of the Highlands, the whisky matures for twelve long years. This fine malt is then ready to be enjoyed by malt whisky lovers the world over.

Overhead at the gates to The Glendronach, rooks fly protectively over tall trees housing a rookery which is said to give good luck to the distillery. It is yet another aspect of the delightful character of this Highland distillery which has given its name to this exceptional malt whisky.

The Distillery is open from September to end of June. Tours available by appointment only. Contact The Glendronach Distillery, Forgue, by Huntly, Aberdeenshire AB5 6DS. Telephone: 046 682 202.

Scotch Whisky, made in Germany, is now being largely imported into India. The wholesale price is sixpence per quart bottle.
     - Vanity Fair, December 1892.

Benromach - Glenlivet letterhead

ON THIS DAY IN DECEMBER...

4th December 1903
- The Elgin Courant announces the sale of Knockando-Glenlivet distillery to Messrs. W. & A. Gilbey Ltd for £3,500.

5th December 1933
- Prohibition is repealed in the U.S.A.

8th December 1837
- Strathisla distillery is advertised for sale by public roup.

10th December 1919
- The Forres Gazette announces that Benromach distillery is to be restored and that distilling is to begin early in 1920.

12th December 1990
- Speyside distillery goes into production.

THE "REAL" THING ?

In London, towards the end of the 19th century, a party of Scots visited a "Scots tryst", and found that the only Scottish thing there was whisky. It may have been made in Germany, but it was labelled "Roderick Dhu".

T he Whisky here is said to have no rival in the world. There are several kinds manufactured, first patent "Grain Whisky", second "Pot Still Irish", third "Silent Malt", and fourth "Flavoured Malt". The annual output is 1,300,000 gallons, but this could be increased if necessary.

- Alfred Barnard describing the produce of Cameron Bridge distillery in Fife, 1887.

COUNTERFEITING

Counterfeiting is a very popular, easy and profitable - for the criminals - way of making money. Copying a product in which another company has invested large sums in research, development and marketing is a cheap way to "cash in".

Whisky is such a product. Not only do the criminals produce replicas of internationally-known brands such as Johnnie Walker, Cutty Sark or Chivas Regal, they also pass off the locally produced spirit as Scotch Whisky.

Admixtures contain a quantity of Scotch Whisky as well as local spirit and it has been argued that it is legitimate to use indications of Scottish origin because the bottle contains a proportion of Scotch Whisky. The Scotch Whisky Association, in its Annual Review of 1986, said "The protection of the geographical meaning of the description "Scotch Whisky" remains of vital importance. If consumers are misled into believing that the word "Scotch" describes simply a type of whisky which can be produced

anywhere, competitors will reap where they have not sown and the reputation of excellence, painstakingly built up by the Industry over many years, will be severely damaged."

PROTECTION OF SCOTCH WHISKY

Throughout the year the Association gave the highest priority to the protection of the description "Scotch Whisky" as an indication of geographical origin. The volume of consequent litigation worldwide continued to increase and the Association was involved in over 70 actions or contemplated actions involving more than 120 brands sold in 24 different countries. A particular problem is the growing number of products which, although not whiskies and not described as whiskies, are nevertheless passed off as Scotch Whiskies.

- The Scotch Whisky Association
Annual Review, 1991.

Gie him strong drink, until he wink.

That's sinking in despair;

And liquor guid tae fire his bluid,

That's prest wi' grief and care;

There let him bouse and deep carouse,

Wi' bumbers flowing o'er,

Till he forgets his loves or debts,

And minds his griefs no more.

- Proverbs 31, verses 6 & 7.

Upper end of the Grange distillery, Burntisland

*Whisky - a little embrocation is comfort for
the soul.*
                              - Anon

Dray horses at Gloag's of Perth

ON THIS DAY IN DECEMBER...

18th December 1889
- A fire at Talisker distillery destroys £2,000 worth of grain and buildings.

22nd December 1989
- Glenfarclas and Cardhu distilleries receive "Loo of the Year" awards for their facilities.

24th December 1841
- The Royal Household orders a cask of "Islay Mountain Dew".

The old mill, which rises from the centre of the Distillery, which has been left standing as a distinguishing feature and a relic of the past, is a landmark for many miles round. It is of solid construction, some 70 feet wide at its base, and rises to the great height of 150 feet. Crowning its summit is a vast cupola, surmounted by a brazen figure of Ireland's patron saint, mitre and crozier in hand. In the olden times this Wind-mill used to supply the entire motive power for the distillery.

> - Alfred Barnard, describing the Thomas Street Distillery, Dublin in 1887.

SURPLUS POWER

Deanston Distillery, near Doune in Perthshire does not have the antiquity of the Thomas Street Distillery, but it does have its own power source. The River Teith, a not inconsequential body of water which, at times of flood can rise very rapidly and considerably in volume, flows past the distillery. Even at times of serious drought it contains a substantial volume of water.

This water-course is tapped and the diverted waters are passed through one of two turbines. These generate more than enough power to run the distillery and the surplus electricity generated is sold to the local electricity generating company.

WILL LLOYD GEORGE FEED THEM?

The next figure in the foreground of this picture after the farmer and agricultural labourer is the distillery worker. He stands at the distillery gates begging for employment and no engagement is obtained. At these 88 distilleries, he and his dependants number 5280 souls. There is no other work open to them. All grooves of skilled and unskilled labour are already filled. He cannot emigrate for he has not the means. Observe him trying to obtain provisions for himself and his starving family at the local grocery store.

The storekeeper is fast approaching the same condition. He has already given him credit in the expectation of a reopening of the distilleries and cannot further extend. What will become of the 5280 souls? Local charity is exhausted. Will Lloyd George feed them?

> - From the *Glasgow Herald*, 23rd September, 1909 after an excessive increase in Excise duty in the 1909 U.K. Budget.

Mill wheel

*In America, whisky has long been considered
a power drink, the sophisticated choice of
middle-aged men on Wall Street or Capitol
Hill.*
                    **- Bill Burdick, Sherlock's Home,
                                   Minnetonka.**

Glenfiddich staff, 1896

ON THIS DAY IN DECEMBER...

25th December 1748
- The wearing of the "plaid, philibeg or little-kilt" is banned on pain of six months'
imprisonment without bail.

25th December 1887
- The first spirit is produced at Glenfiddich.

26th December 1981
- Invergordon Distillers announces plans to convert the old mill at Tomnavoulin into the
visitors' centre at Tamnavulin distillery.

THE GOOD THINGS IN LIFE

Schenley, Dewars' agents in the United States, ran an advertisement which featured an old chap and his collie dog walking through the streets of the village of Culross in Fife. The ad ran the line:

"He was never elected, but every night 'Mayor' Orlo McBain is the last man to walk the streets of Culross, Scotland. He checks a knob, closes a gate and goes on his way. The good things in life stay that way."

Orlo McBain is in fact Ian McLeod, curator of the National Trust for Scotland's many properties in the village, who was approached by a Chicago advertising agency and asked to pose with a borrowed dog. The generous advertising agents donated $100 to the National Trust and gave the dog's owner $25. Ian McLeod still awaits his bottle.

A robber, who thought that he had stolen a bottle of one of the world's most expensive whiskies from a display cabinet in London's Fortnum & Mason store, will have a nasty taste left in his mouth when he samples his ill-gotten dram. What he believed he had stolen was a bottle of Springbank 50 Years Old Single Malt carrying a price tag of £6,750.00. What he in fact stole was a special dummy display bottle containing - vinegar!

ENTERPRISING

White Horse Distillers ran a very enterprising and imaginative series of advertisements in the late 1970s and early 1980s with the copy-line "Whisky and... "

"Whisky and American", for example, featured the company's horse, white of course, and a U.S. basketball player. The horse has featured in many unusual settings over the years: e.g. at a cocktail party on the side of a swimming pool, thus proving that it can be taken anywhere!

Scotch Whisky is about the only thing left that is guaranteed to bring comfort to mankind.

- Lord Boothby in a speech to the House of Lords, 1984.

DEFACEMENT

The Macallan has run a series of pawky advertisements over the years. One such involved Alfred, a barman at the Caledonian Club in London, who refused to allow a Texan visitor to the Club to put ginger ale into 18 years old Macallan. He is quoted as saying, "I'll no' be a party to defacing national monuments!"

Bell's advertising, New York, 1937

The majority of drinkers in the U.K. drink lightly or moderately. There is abundant evidence that such drinkers suffer fewer heart attacks than total abstainers.
                    - The Portman Group.

ON THIS DAY IN DECEMBER...

Carting draft and coal to Rothes station, 1936

27th December 1897
- The Forres Gazette advises that 14 acres on the estate of Sanquhar are "given off" for the purpose of erecting Benromach distillery.

28th December 1897
- Speyburn distillery comes into production.

30th December 1892
- A notice of the sale of Macallan distillery and the "desirable and compact farm" attached to it, to Roderick Kemp of Elgin, appears in the Elgin Courant. This "desirable and compact little farm" is Easter Elchies, the farmhouse of which was magnificently refurbished in 1985 to become the company's corporate headquarters.

ADDRESS TO THE BARLEY SEED

When the Lord first planted oot the earth wi'
trees an' flo'ers an' weeds,

He scattered roon' Speyside a puckle barley
seeds;

Thus was the birth o' Scotia's brew on that
fair springtime morn,

For in the month that followed, John
Barleycorn was born.

The threshin' plant had scarce made off, the
golden grain was cairted,

Syne bags for siller were exchanged an'
industry was started.

O barley seed, had ye but known the fate that
lay before ye,

The very day in which ye breared ye'd ha'e
telt the earth tae smo'er ye.

Regardless o' yer injured pride, yer golden
grains sae gleamin',

They ran ye on conveyor belts that in a steep
were teamin',

An' there ye lay for 'oors on end, sae soakin'
an' sae sodden.

Syne they spread ye oot tae dry, trampled on
and trodden.

Frae there they took ye tae the kiln, ye thocht
they'd only toast ye.

They held on coke an' peats until, ye thocht,
"My God, they'll roast me!"

They sent ye tae the millroom an they hackit
an' they cut ye.

Syne they sent ye aff again, in the Glory Hole
they shut ye.

An' so ye cam' tae the day o' days when the
mashman started mashin';

They pushed ye doon the hopper in tae the
mashtun splashin';

They soaked ye in the bilin' bree an' drained
the watter aff;

They sheeled ye doon the drag hole an' noo
ye're only draff.

O whit a come doon tae yer pride, wee
golden barley seed,

Tae think ye'd land in sic a soss for the sake
o' human greed.

Tae think that once yer golden grains were
shimmerin' in the breeze

An' noo ye're lyin' stinkin', like ony mouldy
cheese.

But ye've ae consolation that canna fail tae
cheer ye,

For noo there's millions love ye, aye, an'
millions also fear ye.

Noo ye're in a bottle, in the world ye stand
supreme -

The world wad gang doon on its knees tae
ye O' Mountain Cream.

They preach ye frae the pulpit, an' mony a
woman's cursed ye,

Aye, an' mony a cheel when he threw the
mash wad cherish ye an' nurse ye.

Ye bring a sparkle tae the e'e, ye also bring a
tear,

Ye've saved a life, ye've caused a death, ye
inspire baith pluck an' fear.

In solace noo, wee barley seed, or is it barley
bree?

I'd like tae say that ilka day my hand gangs
oot for ye,

At seven o' clock each mornin', at five o'
clock each nicht.

If I should fail tae find ye, I'd drap doon
deid wi' fricht.

- Anon, published in *Around The Stills*, the
staff magazine of Scottish Malt Distillers.

*One whisky is alright, two is too much and
three is too few.*

- Old Highland saying.

GLOSSARY OF TERMS

Because of the nature of the Scots language, with its roots in Gaelic, French, Latin and, finally, English, the publishers think that I should include a Glossary of Terms to help you translate some of the stories. Both the publishers and I have gone through the proofs to pick out expressions which you, the reader, might find difficult. I apologise if there are some we have missed.

Half-seas over (page 7)
- under the influence of drink

Guid sneezin' (page 9)
- a good pinch of snuff

Cast oot wi' (page 9)
- fell out with; objected to

Pree (page 13)
- sample; taste

Blither (page 13)
- more joyous; happier

Blee-lang (page 13)
- late; long

Bree (page 13)
- a liquid in which something has been boiled to extract flavours, e.g. stock

Peeched (page 21)
- informed against someone

Leein' (page 23)
- lying; untruthful

Sic (page 25)
- such

Fat (page 29)
- what

Aye (page 29)
- always

Gi'e (page 29)
- give

Launger the war (page 29)
- worse

Daurna (Page 29)
- dare not

Splore (page 29)
- party

Ken (page 33)
- know

Rinnin' (page 33)
- running

Ower (page 33)
- over

Abave (page 37)
- over; above

Takin' tent (page 37)
- taking care

Mauna (page 37)
- cannot

Muckle (page 37)
- much

Compeared (page 43)
- appeared (before a court or other authority such as a church congregation)

Deponed (page 43)
- testified; gave evidence

Reiking (page 43)
- smoking; smelling

Byt presentlie cam'd (page 43)
- recently returned

Nae doot (page 45)
- without doubt

Whaur (page 45)
- where

Maun (page 45)
- must

Meal pock (page 54)
- grain sack

Willy-waught (page 54)

- a good hearty swig (from a glass)

Night cappy (page 54)

- a dram before bed-time

Saycrit (page 56)

- secret

Bittock (page 63)

- a small bit

Canny (page 75)

- careful (with money)

Shump (page 77)

- leap

Bilin' (page 83)

- boiling

Unco (page 87)

- excessively

Criest (page 87)

- shrivelled

Gang (page 89)

- travel; go

Clap (page 97)

- throw (in jail)

Drooned (page 113)

- drowned

Pouch (page 115)

- pocket

Yon (page 119)

- that

Bouse (page 125)

- drink to excess

Carouse (page 125)

- drink (deeply)

Bumbers (page 125)

- a large glass or drinking vessel filled to the brim, usually for toasts

Puckle (page 131)

- little

Cairted (page 131)

- transported; carried off

Syne (page 131)

- soon

Siller (page 131)

- money (silver)

Breared (page 131)

- germinated; appeared above the surface of the soil

Smo'er (page 131)

- smother

Teamin' (page 131)

- running (with water)

'oors (page 131)

- hours

Sodden (page 131)

- boiled; cooked by boiling

Thockt (page 131)

- thought

Hackit (page 131)

- chopped up

Sheeled (page 131)

- husked; taken out of the husk

Soss (page 131)

- a wet, soggy mess of food

Ony (page 131)

- any

Ae (page 131)

- one

Cheel (page 131)

- lad

Pluck (page 131)

- courage

Ilka (page 131)

- every

Fricht (page 131)

- fright

INDEX

The Scotch Whisky Association

The Scotch Whisky Association is the trade association for the Scotch Whisky industry. Its roots go back to the early part of the century and it has existed in its present form since the 1940s.

Headquartered in Edinburgh with an office in London, its role is to promote Scotch Whisky and to watch over its interests. To represent members' views in consultations with Government and to influence legislation or, where necessary, to have it changed or repealed.

The 121 member companies of the Association, all of whom are distillers, blenders, owners of proprietary brands or exporters of Scotch Whisky, together comprise more than 90% of Scotland's blending and distilling capacity.

The aims of the Association are:

To protect and promote the interests of the Industry at home and abroad. To originate, promote, support or oppose legislative or other measures directly or indirectly affecting the Industry.

To enter into legal proceedings in any part of the world in defence of the interests of the Industry.

To collect statistical and other information relating to the Industry and to supply members with such information.

The Secretariat at the Edinburgh office provides a variety of commercial and legal services and advice to member companies. It collects and disseminates information on export requirements, tariffs and other regulations in all the world markets to which Scotch Whisky is shipped. It is also responsible for initiating legal actions against whiskies that are produced in many parts of the world and passed off fraudulently as Scotch.

The S.W.A. runs public relations campaigns, aimed at promoting the image of Scotch Whisky as an up-scale prestige drink.